OUT
EAST

OUT
EAST

MEMOIR OF A MONTAUK SUMMER

JOHN
GLYNN

GRAND CENTRAL
PUBLISHING

NEW YORK   BOSTON

Copyright © 2019 by John Glynn
Cover design by TK. Cover copyright © 2019 by Hachette Book Group, Inc.

Grand Central Publishing
Hachette Book Group
1290 Avenue of the Americas, New York, NY 10104
grandcentralpublishing.com
twitter.com/grandcentralpub

First Edition: May 2019

Grand Central Publishing is a division of Hachette Book Group, Inc. The Grand Central Publishing name and logo is a trademark of Hachette Book Group, Inc.

The publisher is not responsible for websites (or their content) that are not owned by the publisher.

The Hachette Speakers Bureau provides a wide range of authors for speaking events. To find out more, go to www.hachettespeakersbureau.com or call (866) 376-6591.

Library of Congress Cataloging-in-Publication Data has been applied for.

ISBNs: 978-1-5387-4665-3 (hardcover), 978-1-5387-4664-6 (ebook)

Printed in the United States of America

LSC-C

10 9 8 7 6 5 4 3 2 1

For my mom and dad

AUTHOR'S NOTE

The events of this memoir took place during a flexion point in my life. To cross-check my memories, I combed through a digital footprint of photos, emails, text messages, Gchats, and social media posts. But I never could have constructed this book without the generosity of my Montauk housemates. The individuals who appear in these pages gifted me their thoughts, experiences, and secrets from that summer. They revealed aspects of their lives to me I never before knew. Any liberties in perspective are animated by these conversations and grounded in the facts as they were relayed to me. Errors are solely my own. In some instances I changed names or identifying characteristics to protect anonymity. I hope I've done our story justice.

While Montauk became our sanctuary, we resided there only at the pleasure of its locals. My indelible gratitude to the people of Montauk, in particular Calli and Lindsay Stavola, who read this memoir with a keen local eye. Thank you to the entire community for sharing your sand-swept home with us at a time when we needed it most.

WINTER

Chapter One

Our summer began in the winter.

Chauvin bought the tree, and Evan hung the lights. I wrote the Facebook invitation and sent it to eighty-six people. We lashed a wreath to the door. We adhered stockings to the walls with duct tape.

Caroline and Charlotte were making red and green Jell-O shots. Lizzie was bringing three handles of Svedka. We spent the day vacuuming, scrubbing, dusting, and by six p.m. our three-bedroom apartment, glinting, immaculate, was warming with scents of pine and cinnamon and the cloying multipurpose cleaner we used to polish every surface.

We lived in Tribeca on a windswept portion of Greenwich Street. Out our windows we could see a sushi den, a dive bar, and a coffee shop owned by Hugh Jackman. Our building was a brick high-rise—thirty-four floors, concrete accents, the brutalist design at odds with the modern lofts and converted warehouses around it. To us the apartment was an acropolis, one we occupied by stupid luck. The amenities were beyond our scope of experience: stainless steel appliances, blond hardwood floors, a bathroom with a shower wand. A door opened to a private terrace off our living room with views of downtown Manhattan. Each morning we stepped outside and watched the Freedom Tower rise up pane by pane—first a pole of spires and stents, then a half-dressed obelisk, then, with its glass coats spiraling to the top day by day, a patriotic mirror in the sky.

At eight p.m. the ice company arrived with a carved ice luge. Two men in Carhartt jackets wheeled it to the terrace and removed the cold block from a taped-up blanket.

"This is the seventh one we've delivered tonight," said one of the men to my roommate Chauvin.

"And here we thought we were special!" he replied.

The man pressed a button and the luge lit up. The words *Merry Christmas* glowed in a pantheon of dissolving colors.

"You are," he said.

It was unseasonably mild that night—fifty-five degrees, humid, a light mist ghosting the street. Our apartment was dim and cozy, illuminated only by the Christmas lights that we'd strung across the ceiling. I poured cider into a pot on the stove. Chauvin added rum and cinnamon sticks. We set up the beer pong table in the foyer and moved the coffee table for dancing. Hung mistletoe for good luck.

Evan and Chauvin both had girlfriends. I figured I'd find someone soon.

I didn't have my eye on anyone in particular that night. Since moving to the city I had hooked up with a handful of girls and quasi-dated one. Her name was Shelly. It was short-lived and she unfriended me on Facebook.

Still, we were all at the age where dating felt real. Friends were pairing off, staying in, rising early, signing leases. Marriage, kids, thoughts of the suburbs. The previous summer I'd attended seven weddings. I ate seven plates of chicken française and danced to "Shout" seven times. I watched seven mothers dance with their sons.

I drank.

I drank gin and tonics on the lawns of country clubs and flutes of champagne through awkward toasts. I guzzled wine by the globeful, making small talk with the bride's camp friend, the groom's coworker, the cousins from Kentucky whom I'd never see again. Before the dancing I ordered shots, or if shots weren't on offer I ordered tequila neat. I'd kick the liquor back in one mouth-smacking swill, ready to have the best night of my life.

It was 9:15 and our guests were supposed to arrive at 9:30. I always got nervous before throwing parties, but that night my anxiety—which had steadily increased over the past few years—grew volcanic. I darted to the bathroom, fixing my hair, tucking and untucking my flannel shirt, smiling at my reflection, breathing against the drumbeat inside my head. Chauvin wore a blazer. Should I wear a blazer? I decided to borrow one of his ties.

I checked my phone compulsively. My nerves crackled. Nine thirty-five. Nine forty. I sent a few desperate texts. Where are you? You guys still coming? I glommed my eye to the peephole, blinking into our empty hallway, the sight of the warped walls and doors instilling within me a silent dread.

The three of us tested the ice luge on the balcony while we waited. The peppermint schnapps a cold river. I did two in a row before I heard the doorbell.

"Finally!" Evan said. "Someone's here."

I went back inside and opened the door.

"Johnny Drama!"

It was my college roommate Mike and his boyfriend, Shane. I ushered them to the kitchen, admiring their tweed blazers. Christmas, with its bright color palette and decorous wardrobe, was the ideal showcase for their coupledom. Their hair was perfectly coiffed, their cheeks pink and smooth. They seemed to exist on a different life plane, one where people wore woven belts and vintage watches.

"The apartment looks amazing!" Mike said. "I'm normally a white lights person but I love the colors."

I took his coat and offered him a drink. "We've got vodka, tequila, wine, whiskey, beer. Everything the light touches."

"Tequila soda? Two limes."

I opened the Patrón.

Mike, Evan, and I went out to the ice luge. The three of us had formed a triumvirate in college, but Mike stood at the center, the cruise director of our social group. He organized pregames, bar crawls, birthday parties, and spring breaks.

College, for Mike, had been about building relationships. Academics were secondary to establishing his network. While Evan and I scrolled through our textbooks, highlighters in hand, Mike was playing *Legend of Zelda* with the guys down the hall.

Even when he wanted to study, he struggled to focus. Before an exam he'd pop an Adderall, only to waste the high manically rearranging his dorm room. As college progressed his mind grew unsettled. He'd lock himself in his room with a jug of wine and wouldn't come out until he had finished it. An inner conflict was blooming within him.

When Evan and I came back from studying abroad our junior year, Mike had lost eighty pounds, dyed his hair, and come out of the closet. He no longer drank jugs of wine by himself. Over the course of his final two semesters, we watched him make up for lost time.

On the balcony, Mike took a shot on the ice luge and lit a cigarette. Then he shut the door.

"I want to talk to you guys about something. Before too many people get here." He was peering into the living room, his hands tremoring, and it immediately dawned on me what he was going to say. Mike and Shane had been dating for five years, their lives like locked magnets. They were getting engaged. I braced myself for the announcement, prepping my reaction. I would be thrilled for him, of course, but the news would inevitably kick up my own feelings of loneliness. My friends were moving forward, but the slides of my own life weren't coming together.

I summoned my most enthusiastic voice. "So when's it happening?"

Mike looked confused. "When's what happening?"

"The proposal."

"What proposal?"

"When are you popping the question?"

"Wait, what? Did you think this was *that* conversation? Oh my God, no."

We all laughed.

"Don't get me wrong, I love Shane, but we're not there yet. I wanted to talk to you guys about Montauk."

7

I felt a wash of relief. Each engagement signaled a further un-winding of the plurality that had defined us since college. But Montauk, the beach town at the end of Long Island, nodded toward adventure, connection. A delayed pursuit of more adult concerns. Mike had organized a share house there the previous summer. I felt my nerves unclench as he explained.

"We have a few extra spots. The girls are doing their house, too. It would make my life if you guys did it."

I'd witnessed the exodus the summer before—a vanishing from Friday to Sunday, then a weeklong recuperation period in which my friends declined to go out. I lived vicariously through their sun-washed photos, noting the influx of new faces. A single share cost two thousand dollars, which, according to Mike, was much cheaper than hotels.

"It's like summer camp for adults," he said. "There's this bar called Ruschmeyer's that plays Motown on Friday nights, and this new place called the Surf Lodge. Plus we spend all day on the beach."

After one summer in New York, the idea of escaping Man-hattan's pillared heat held immense appeal. I'd grown up going to the Connecticut shore and loved the ocean. But I knew it wasn't feasible. I definitely didn't have two thousand dollars.

"Well, just think about it, okay? You too, Evan."

Mike turned back to admire our Christmas tree. The white lights reflected against our collection of dollar-store ornaments. "Is that a Fraser fir?" he asked. "It looks like a Fraser fir."

By eleven, our apartment was a weave of color. Sixty people swiveled through our halls and onto the dance floor. I controlled the music, doled out Jell-O shots, and tossed fresh beers across the room. Little flocks of guests gathered in the bedrooms for secret conversations and other, more illicit things. I downed two more Jell-O shots and played a round of beer pong, losing terribly. The classics echoed through the speakers—Brenda Lee, Darlene Love, Bing Crosby, and José Feliciano. Mariah Carey's "All I Want for Christmas Is You" came on and everyone belted. It came on three more times.

I heard a knock on the door and flung it open. It was Paul, another one of my friends from college and a close Gchat confidant. Like Mike, he was gay. He stood there with a kid I knew peripherally.

"John, you remember Fred, right?"

Fred was the year below me in college. We hadn't known each other back then, but our New York circles overlapped a bit. I'd seen him around.

"What's up, man?"

He wore a red knitted sweater with white snowflakes and fitted corduroys from J.Crew. He wasn't short, but he seemed compact. A square jaw, square head, thick-cropped jet-black hair.

"Good to see you again!"

We awkwardly went in for a bro-tap handshake. His black eyes were glazed and roving, breath infused with the buttery scent of Fireball. I brought him and Paul to the kitchen and told them to help themselves. The music toggled from holiday classics to dancing songs. Ke$ha's "Die Young" was popular that winter, and it started to play on repeat.

This was where I thrived, in the moments of haze: the dancing, the music, the collective buzz. Chaos was intimacy; distraction was intimacy. Watching a friend do blow off the dresser was intimacy. My parents were in the city that weekend, staying in a hotel in SoHo. They were planning to swing by our apartment after their nine p.m. dinner at the Odeon. Long enough to say hi to my friends, have a drink, take in the scene. My mom would consume exactly one glass of chardonnay and my dad would play a single game of beer pong. Then they'd go back to their room and call me the next morning to tell me how much they loved my New York life. They were the fun parents, the most beloved. We had a wonderful relationship, and I was proud to have them.

I dipped out to the terrace for some fresh air. A few people were smoking cigarettes by the Christmas tree. A fog rolled along Greenwich Street, gauzing the Freedom Tower in an ethereal glow. Fred walked out.

"Dude! An ice luge."

I grabbed the schnapps and offered him a pour. He crouched down, pressing his lips to the iced track.

"You're not gonna do one with me?"

I called over my friend Gabi, who was smoking a Newport in the corner. She grabbed the Fireball in one hand and the schnapps in the other. I knelt down, placed my bottom lip against the other track.

"Ready?" Fred asked. Our faces were touching.

I gave the thumbs-up and Gabi poured.

The Fireball slashed through my mouth. Fred finished the schnapps and gasped, eyes watering.

"That was epic."

Gabi went back inside and Fred and I stayed out on the terrace. He told me how he'd come from a gay pregame with Paul. He was new to the scene and still trying to carve a foothold. Out of nerves, he'd drunk more than he'd intended. He was relieved to be back with his college support system.

"I love my Boston College friends. They're like, the best, man. They've been so great to me."

"That's awesome. I love my BC friends, too."

"Why aren't you gay?" he asked.

I thought I misheard him.

"Huh?"

"I mean, I know you're not gay. But why aren't you?"

A smile stretched across his face. Beneath my skin I felt something like tectonic plates shifting.

"What?"

"I wish you were."

"Why?"

"Because I like you. And we could be together."

I stared straight ahead. The glowing apartments across the way burned through the fog.

I gave him a friendly shove.

"You're drunk," I said. "Too many luges."

"It's like...the Winter Olympics."

I heard a commotion inside. My parents had arrived.

My mom, Thomasina—that was her name and she'd earned every letter of it—wore a crimson leather jacket. At sixty-two she was still a fashion plate. Blond hair, genetically gifted skin, active and fit. She could pass for forty-five.

"My parents are here. I should go back inside," I said to Fred.

My mom saw me through the living room window and let out a hyena-like yip.

"Johnny!"

We had been together over Thanksgiving, but I still missed

them all the time. My dad trailed behind my mom, folding his glasses into his coat pocket. He gave me a hug. As the girls swarmed my mom, my dad pulled me aside.

"Is that a BC bud?" he asked, nodding to Fred. "I don't recognize him!"

"Oh, him?" I said, heart stammering in an unfamiliar way. "He's no one."

Chapter Two

Shortly after Christmas, Kicki died. She was my last living grandparent, my mom's mom. She'd outlived my grandfather by a year. She died in her own bed, in the in-law apartment above my aunt Ellen's house, just down the street from my parents.

In her final hours we surrounded her, clutching styrofoam cups of Dunkin' Donuts coffee. Kicki was our matriarch. My cousins and I worshipped her.

I went back to Massachusetts for the funeral, but in my grief left my suit bag on the train. It had contained my jacket, dress pants, shirt, tie, and belt. My dad raced me up to the Jos. A. Bank before it closed. Then he called Vladimir's Tailors and convinced them to open early the next day, a Saturday, to hem the pants first thing.

I hated myself for losing the suit bag, and my dad's instinct to kindness only accentuated my sense of ineptitude, my inability to be an adult. He was a good man and a problem solver. I felt like a hot mess.

The next day I was ablaze with insecurity. I felt awkward in the new suit and worried it was too large and boxy. I tended to avoid wearing formal clothes in general because they made me feel like an imposter, a kid playing dress-up. I processed down the aisle, the pages of my eulogy tucked in my pocket.

I took a seat in the pew next to my cousin Jay. He was a year younger than me. We'd gone to the same middle and high schools and were best buds. He was going to deliver a eulogy, too.

I remember standing at the lectern, hands trembling, staring out at the two hundred or so people who filled the church, but I have no memory of the speech itself. Instead I have an overmemory. I'm sitting in the pew, watching myself deliver the eulogy. I'm separate from the person in the pulpit. I am not that person. That is not who I am. I am the person in the last row, by the door.

There were sixteen of us, and we arrived in three waves. Four older cousins, eight in the middle, and three babies at the end.

I was the middle of the middle, a fall baby, born on the feast day of Saint Jude. When I was a kid my mom encouraged me to pray to him. He was the patron saint of hopeless cases, and I absorbed his iconography. Every year during the last week of October, Holy Name Church in Springfield held a weeklong novena in Saint Jude's honor. My mother attended each night after dinner, sometimes with a sister or two, often with Kicki. One evening my mom brought me back a prayer card. On one side stood Saint Jude, haloed and barefoot in an emerald meadow. On the other, a Catholic prayer, which I read while kneeling. I tacked the card to my corkboard and asked Saint Jude to intercede when I needed it.

I held a liberal interpretation of hopeless cases and often prayed for frivolous things. A win for my basketball team. A Super Nintendo. An A on a science test I hadn't studied for. But mostly, at night, I prayed for a sibling.

I was an only child, the only only child I knew. At five I wrote a story, dictated to my mom and illustrated by me in Magic Marker, called "The Wishing Turtle." In it, the Wishing Turtle wishes for "another him." One day, as the wishing turtle is basking by his lake, another him appears in the water. The two meet and are instantly inseparable. They play a game called "splash the knocky turtle" and are together forever. The end.

Even at five I was thinking about the mystic connection one could discover in another. The idea that you could travel through life with someone seemed to me like the zenith of happiness. Life, like a double-sticked popsicle, was meant to be cracked down the middle. Here, I'd say. One half for you, one half for me. Red's my favorite flavor, too. When you finish, keep the stick. There's a joke written on it.

My mom had me when she was thirty-five. She got pregnant again at thirty-seven. In a beach photo she wears a loose nautical shirt, her body freckled and lithe save for the smallest melon forming beneath her hand. I'm holding on to her leg in my diaper. There was a miscarriage. I don't know if my parents tried again.

The eight cousins in the middle had been born in a three-year cluster, and of those eight, seven were boys. In the summers we were herded through life together. Each morning we swam at the town pool, competing for Red Cross cards and pieces

15

of bubble gum wrapped with stick-on tattoos. My mom and aunts took turns making lunch. Eight PB&Js lined across the table. Eight small glasses of 2 percent milk.

On Fridays we had cousin sleepovers and watched *Indiana Jones* and *Home Alone* in my aunt Ellen's attic. We ate pizza and washed it down with orange soda. At bedtime we rolled our sleeping bags across the attic floor and sang the theme song from *Stone Protectors*.

As the others drifted to sleep, I'd lie awake, breathing in the scents of my pillow from home. The windows were open and my ears were like conch shells, amplifying every noise: crickets and joggers, insects battering the screen. Then the baleful moan of a distant train, a sound that, for reasons I didn't understand, made me miss my mom, my own bed, my stuffed animals and blanket. I snuggled next to my cousins, even in the heat, and tried to be brave.

I was in a pig pile, physically surrounded, yet somehow I felt dislocated. Different. I didn't understand the loneliness. I just knew it was there. Like the moon gone dark.

The next morning there was a rush of light. My cousins yawned and stretched and cracked their ankles. The air had gone cooler, a dew clung to the screen. I felt a jolt of anticipation knowing my mom would pick me up in a few hours. Everything was better in the morning, even the leftover brownies, which Ellen let us eat off the pan with our cereal because she was the youngest, hippest aunt.

Kicki had come over that morning, too, and was sipping tea from a clear mug. She watched us eat and feigned concern.

"Oh my word. Brownies for breakfast. What will your mothers think?"

Our mothers shared the same maternal gaze. They were the Kelliher sisters—five of them, one in each grade, the loud laughers, the popular ones. They had all been champion synchronized swimmers. Good girls. Bad Catholics. They'd grown up with nothing, but had all they needed.

My mom was the fourth girl. Named Thomasina, Thom for short, because my grandfather's name was Thomas, and my grandparents were certain they'd never have a son (they did two years later, my uncle Jim, whom everyone called Kell). Growing up she disliked her name, but she eventually learned to love it. In a town of Barbaras and Lindas, she was a Beyoncé. But I was given a short, plain, one-syllable name for a reason.

My mom met my dad while jogging in Forest Park. A game of tennis followed, along with a trip to Friendly's for ice cream sundaes. In a scratched booth, over scoops of chocolate chip, my dad explained that he had just gotten into medical school in Italy. In six months he'd be moving to Perugia. He didn't know the language and could barcly afford a plane ticket. My mom was sold. Three days later, they were engaged.

My mom went to Casual Corner, a discount store at the Holyoke Mall. She found a white dress on the clearance rack and it became her wedding dress. She wore a wreath of flowers in her hair.

They spent one winter curled up on a kitchen floor in Perugia, sleeping as close as they could to the open oven, too poor to afford an apartment with heat. But they were young and beautiful and in love; the vagaries of the world faded to ether.

This was my foundational narrative. The master truth that shaped all the others. Love hits you instantly, effortlessly, and all at once. It never fades, it never changes, it endures forever, and it defines you. When you find that person, you push your chips all in.

You just know.
  You just know.
  You just know.

Thirty-five years later—my dad now a successful oncologist, my mom an elementary school teacher—they were still wildly in love. They'd come from nothing and built a life together. They had raised a child who wanted for nothing, gave him a small-town childhood, a house with a backyard, a driveway with a basketball hoop, a bicycle, a car. And now he lived in the city, in Tribeca, where Robert De Niro and Jay-Z lived, and he worked for a publishing company, and went to concerts, and spotted famous people on the street. When his grandmother died, he delivered her eulogy.

They had been good parents. They deserved a happy son.

Chapter Three

On the Friday of MLK weekend we drove up to Stratton, Vermont. My friend Caroline's parents had a condo by the mountain, and they let us use it often. There were seven of us heading up in three separate cars. I was in the late-departing car with my friend Billy.

Billy and I stopped at my parents' house in Longmeadow, Massachusetts, so I could pick up my skis. My mom handed us a bag of Nestlé Crunches, Goldfish, and cans of soda. Our house, a white colonial with green shutters, sat on the corner of a busy street, but the neighborhood was glazed with the kind of silence that only accompanies heavy snowfall.

"Drive safely!" my mom implored through the window.

"Don't worry, Thom! We'll be safe," said Billy.

"Tell Caroline and all the BC buds I say hi! And no driving after après. Love you both!"

We drove through Springfield and got off at exit 6 for Dunkin' Donuts. I ordered a large iced coffee and Billy got a sausage biscuit. After Amherst, civilization started to peel away. We passed Hatfield, Whately, Greenfield, Northfield, towns seemingly built for darkness and solitude. The world of *Ethan Frome* and perpetual winter, towns tinted blue.

A Talking Heads song came on, the lyrics meshing with my coiled thoughts. *How did I get here*. My mind wandered back to our Christmas party and my conversation with Fred. He had told me he liked me. He had said that if I were gay, we could be together. I imagined what that would look like. Being together. Not just with Fred, but with anyone. When I thought about love I had to track back to high school, to an ethereal polevaulter, a girl named Jodi. During her track practice I'd watch as Jodi lofted to the sky, her legs pale and weightless, her mind unburdened, her bone-thin body knifing through the clouds. I'd gaze out from the tennis courts, halting my own practice to peer through the chain link. Jodi and I went to every school dance together. We were best friends but dated other people, lost our virginity to other people. When we finally hooked up senior year, it felt like a terminus. I'd expected the encounter to raze my life and rearrange it, to form a foundation upon which everything else would balance. Physically it was great, but no different from any other hookup. I pictured the pole-vaulting bar, the vault pit, the blue cushioned mat. We'd cleared the hurdle and landed safely on the other side. That was that. Back in line. *Same as it ever was. Same as it ever was.*

I'd never been in a long-term relationship, though I'd wanted one desperately. As my friends paired off I'd started to wonder why I wasn't connecting. The answer was I had no idea, and the not knowing was what kept me up at night.

Billy and I got to the condo around 10:15. A crackling fire warmed the great room, drenching its vaulted walls in long shadows. Everyone was drinking big glasses of malbec.

"You made it!" Caroline cheered as we took off our Bean boots. "Bring your stuff upstairs, you guys are in the Animal Room with Shane."

Shane always came to Vermont solo, without Mike. Mike wasn't much of a skier, but Shane loved the outdoors. The rugged opulence of Vermont suited him.

The Animal Room had three adjoining bunk beds dressed in Ralph Lauren blankets. I changed into sweatpants and a Red Sox T-shirt and joined the others downstairs. Shane fed the fire with dry birch, the flames glinting off the moose antlers on the mantel.

"Who wants to smoke?" someone asked.

I donned my boots and went out to the deck. Shivering, huddling, no coats, we breathed in the weed until it cherried. Evan's girlfriend Lizzie cupped the bowl from the wind. The cold air made it impossible to distinguish between the pot smoke and our frosty breath. I felt the high slipping down my arms, narcotizing every muscle.

"I feel like Jack from *Titanic* when he's in the water," I said.

"He could've gotten on that goddamn slab of wood," said Evan. "Lizzie, you remind me of Rose. So high-maintenance."

"Shut up, I am not!"

"Shane, you're definitely Rose's mom," I joked. "And Caroline's the Unsinkable Molly Brown."

"Who are you?" Caroline asked me.

"I'd say I'm Jack because I'm definitely in steerage. But I can't draw. So I'm probably the Italian sidekick. Or the guy who hits his head on the propeller."

Between the red wine and the weed (I rarely smoked), I felt, as I stared into the fire, a deep, battering acceleration of time. I closed my eyes and I was five years old. I opened them and I was twenty-seven. I closed them again and I was forty. I opened them and I was seventy-eight. My life was hurtling by without me, and the intense compression ignited a sense of dread. I felt the sudden need to drink more aggressively.

"Let's play Kings."

It was a passive, slow-moving drinking game, perfect for a big group. We'd played it often in college, usually as part of a pregame. Caroline found cards and fanned them in a circle. We went all the way through the deck.

The next morning Shane drove to the general store for bacon, eggs, and avocados. Caroline made a scramble. We drank mugs of strong coffee. By nine thirty we were in line for the chairlift.

We were all strong skiers, so we stuck to the black diamonds, which were less crowded. I dashed my edges into the snow, feeling the burn in my quads and hamstrings. The wind howled through my teeth, stabbed through the vent in my goggles, whipped my lift ticket against my jacket. We skied as a loose pack, stopping only when the trails converged. Skiing was, in the end, a solitary sport.

We pushed hard through the day and then it was après. At Grizzly's bar I had four Long Trails, two Fireball shots, and the rest of Caroline's Bloody Mary. I spotted a girl from high school I'd lifeguarded with sitting two tables away. Back then some kids had styled a March Madness–type bracket for girls in our high school. Everyone voted online for who they thought was the hottest. The girl at the table had been a one seed. I didn't say hi.

Back at the house I consumed two bottles of red wine with dinner and smoked more weed on the deck. I played beer pong. I played Kings. I played Never Have I Ever. I played music and we danced around the living room. By the time we found a cab that would pick us up, I was nearly nonverbal.

I remember entering the Red Fox Inn, and I remember the bar. I remember thinking our city clothes made us stand out. I remember believing that, since Kicki's death, nothing really mattered one way or the other. I remember a tequila shot. Two tequila shots. And many small bags of Doritos clothespinned and hanging from a string. You could buy them for a dollar. I must have eaten some.

The next thing I remember was the light murdering my eyes in the Animal Room. The smell of bacon. Caroline telling Evan to make coffee.

The hangover radiated from the back of my neck. I was exhausted, but too nauseous to sleep. The idea of getting ready for skiing seemed impossible. My mouth was parched. I went to the kitchen for water.

"Look who's alive!"

I felt a hot sting of embarrassment. I matted down my hair. "What the hell happened last night?" I asked. "I haven't been that drunk since college."

"You. Were. A mess. Like, you couldn't even stand." Caroline was smiling, at least, as she told me this. She was laughing.

"Oh no. Was I really that bad?"

"We all were. Cassie passed out on the bar. Courtney called someone a peasant. We met these two cousins and they started making out with each other. It was fucking weird."

I remembered none of this.

"I don't know if I can go skiing today," I said.

"You're going fucking skiing."

"My head is pounding."

"Take a Tylenol."

I forced down some eggs and drank two cups of coffee. A thermometer suctioned to the window read twelve degrees. As I slipped my snow pants on, I heard my grandfather's voice in my head: *If you want to dance, you gotta pay the fiddler.*

We drove to the mountain in two cars—Caroline's and Billy's. I was in Caroline's car. A fresh layer of snow dusted the trees. With every turn I fought the urge to vomit. My friends didn't seem to have this problem.

Why did I get wrecked like this? I drank to have fun, to slow my anxious thoughts, to amplify my humor. But mostly I drank to connect. I wanted to feel a part of something. I wanted to be loved. I longed for someone to know me in all the ways I couldn't know myself. But the drinking didn't always get me there. It often netted out at oblivion. As we peeled up to the mountain, I wondered if I was the only one in the world who felt like this.

I lasted four runs. I was too sick. I leaned over my poles—heart pulsing, legs sore, a headache crenellating the grooves of my skull. I begged Caroline to let me take her Jeep back. I needed to lie on the couch, watch reality shows, and recuperate. I could meet them later for après.

I carried my skis through the resort, avoiding eye contact with the throngs of families whose bundled wholesomeness amplified my hangover. At the car I sloughed off my coat. I hadn't brought shoes. I removed my ski boots and began to drive in my socks.

I came to the top of a hill and decelerated. The roads were steep and narrow and canalled with big snow banks. I was, for the most part, a cautious driver. I slowed to about ten miles per hour and passed through a covered bridge. I continued downhill, the tires sloshing. On the right side of the road was a steep drop-off with no guardrail. At the next bend, I guided the wheel, but it didn't respond.

Time elasticized. The back tires fishtailed and floated, the steering wheel stopped responding. I could feel the whole car careening to the right, then skidding to the left. The brakes weren't working. I had lost all control. It happened in stop motion, my vision flickering. Ahead I could see the sharp drop and a telephone pole.

My only thought, as the car slid off the road, just before it flipped over: *This can't be it.*

The Jeep was at rest, tipped over on the passenger side. I was still buckled and hanging sideways, in full-body shock. Somehow I managed to stand up with my feet on the passenger window. I pushed the driver's door upward and climbed out of the car as one might ascend a manhole. I was still in my socks.

The car was totaled. I was numb and shaking, but had not

been hurt. If the car had skidded a few inches to the right, it would've struck the telephone pole, and I would have died.

There had to be more, I thought. That couldn't have been it. That couldn't have been my whole life, over before it started. There had to be something more.

Chapter Four

The next week, at work, I received an email with the subject "Montauk." It was from Mike. He had sent it to five of our BC friends.

I worked as an editorial assistant at Scribner, one of the oldest publishing imprints in the city. Our office was located in Rockefeller Center, around the corner from where they filmed *The Today Show*. In nicer weather I could hear the muted roar of the summer concert series. I had grown up watching *The Today Show* and still tuned in as I got ready every morning. To a younger me, this job, in this location, would have been the fulfillment of all my dreams. New York was the hub of the world, and I was there.

Over my lunch break I opened Mike's email. One of my bosses came over as I chomped into my PB&J, asking for a list of sales figures and comparative titles for a potential acquisition. I loved both my bosses and sponged up everything I could from them. They were generous about pulling me into the editorial process, including me on emails with high-profile authors and soliciting my feedback on manuscripts. I admired them professionally, but also liked them as people, and I felt the same level of kinship with my other coworkers. But I hadn't told any of them about Vermont.

Beyond the deep currents of guilt I felt for destroying a friend's car, the accident had dislodged something dark within me. I was emotionally unmoored, immensely mortal. Perils lurked around every corner. I pictured being pushed onto the subway tracks or falling off a happy hour roof deck. I went to bed each night afraid that I would die in my sleep. I began to move through the world with a heightened sense of urgency.

The one reason I was alive, I believed, was because of my grandmother. I sensed she had placed a force field around the car, shrouding me from injury. I began a silent dialogue with Kicki, asking her for help. I felt a pressing need to figure things out, and a crippling inability to do so.

I looked up sales figures for four debut coming-of-age novels with male appeal. My boss was considering a manuscript by an author named Nickolas Butler. The novel was called *Shotgun Lovesongs*. I had read it in one night and loved it. I emailed my boss the sales units. Then I returned to Mike's email.

Hey Guys,

So we just got a call from our Montauk share house owner, and she's gotten multiple offers on her house for well over the price we paid last year. I spoke to our realtor and I guess the market is the most competitive it's ever been.

The owner offered us a first-right-of-refusal, for a *very* reasonable price if we committed by this Sunday.

I don't really have the time to look for another house, and I don't want to risk this not materializing. Caroline, Charlotte, and the rest of the girls are doing a share house again too, so most of our friends will be out there every weekend.

I wanted to gauge your interest now. It will most likely be 25-30 people and the price would be $2,000 for a half share (8 weekends).

I want to manage expectations though. The house is large and can accommodate a lot of people. But occasionally you may have to share a bed or sleep on an air mattress. The house is equipped with a large back deck, a grill, a pool with a diving board and slide. I assume at least 20 people will want to return from last year, which leaves a few open spots. Email me if you'd be interested.

I strongly encourage you to do this because I think you'd have a lot of fun and meet some awesome people in our house.

Let me know,

Mike

That afternoon our managing editor, Perrie, came by my desk. She was from the Philadelphia Main Line. Her best friend from college had grown up with my friend Mike. We had discovered the coincidence the summer before. Perrie had been in the share house and planned to do it again.

"John, I'm telling you. It's the most fun thing ever. You need to do it. Everyone in the house will love you."

Perrie was switch-thin, elegant, and constantly cold. She nestled into a long gypsy sweater festooned with cinches. She had bright red hair, like Mike. The summer before, they'd pretended to be siblings.

"Mike sent me an email today," I said. "He said there are a few open spots."

"I'm telling you. It's summer camp for adults."

"That's exactly what Mike said. I like the idea of meeting new people."

"Remember in college how you'd wake up on Saturdays hungover and everyone would meet in someone's common room and you'd just piece together the night before and laugh and feel connected? That's what it's like every day."

I'd been to Montauk twice since college—sun-slathered weekend trips for friends' birthdays. The beaches were sweeping and majestic, and the town had a surfery charm. But in the wake of the accident I didn't feel worthy of such a privilege. Plus I didn't have the money. I'd sacrificed a savings account and any temporary shot at financial independence for a dream job in a dream city. My parents already helped me with rent. I couldn't ask them for more.

The days grew colder, the dim light of winter battering down. My friends slipped into hibernation. I went to bed earlier each night, seeking refuge in sleep before the waves of anxiety struck me. The walls of my bedroom seemed to shrink. The ceiling compressed.

At night my thoughts turned dark: I was surrounded by friends, but deeply lonely. Time seemed to pass with no meaning. I worried that life would only get worse. That all the good things—friends, family, nice apartment, good job—would eventually disappear, and I would be left with nothing. I was single because there was something wrong with me. Something hardwired into my DNA. Something I didn't know how to fix. Either that or I wasn't good-looking. Or couldn't feign confidence. Or if not one of those things, then something less tangible, some invisible force that veiled my whole being and was entirely exclusive to me. I would die alone. I would never find love. I hadn't before and never would. I would grow old and be poor and have no one and this would all happen quickly, because life accelerates, just look. Yesterday I was seventeen and now I was twenty-seven.

Thoughts like this occurred without warning, snatching my breath. I attributed them to a nameless ineptitude, an inability to connect with anyone on a profound level. They'd first begun in the months after college. Once they came on I was incapable of rerouting them.

I propped my laptop on a pillow, opened Netflix, and pressed play on *The Dick Van Dyke Show*. Rob had just brought home two baby chicks for Richie.

In the past two years I had watched every single episode of *The Dick Van Dyke Show* multiple times. The black-and-white frames sedated me. Each episode followed a set structure of chaste jokes, marital banter, and physical humor. The formula numbed me like Novocain. I lay there, bathed in the glow of my screen. It was the only way I could fall asleep.

Chapter Five

A week later, I received a card in the mail.

My grandmother, living rent-free at my aunt's in-law apartment, had managed to accrue a small nest egg in her last few years of life. Her life savings were divided evenly among the sixteen grandchildren.

My mom sent me a Hallmark card with a note explaining the inheritance.

Tucked in the card was a check for $2,000.

I called her immediately. I told her about Montauk.

"Use it for the share," she said without hesitation.

"I shouldn't save it?"

"Use it for the share. Kicki would have wanted you to."

Almost a month had passed, and I still thought about her every day. Kicki visited me in my dreams, and in dream-soaked memories. From the ages of two to five, we lived above her and my grandfather Pop-Pop in a two-family house in Springfield. Kicki would chase me around the chain-link-fenced backyard, playing hide-and-go-seek and Spud. I ran everywhere, even inside.

Occasionally, on rainy days, Kicki could entice me to sit still. In her TV room we'd unclasp a *Sesame Street* playset comprising a storefront, a functional mailbox, and a two-floor apartment. The plastic rooms were filled with Fisher-Price Little People— hard peg figurines each the size of a thumb. We game-pieced the people up the stairs and down the sidewalks, building out their stories and constructing small worlds. Kicki never tired of my make-believe games.

She was my first best friend.

My mom read to me before bed each night—*The Runaway Bunny*, *Mickey Meets the Giant*, a Little Golden Book called *The Ginghams*—always pairing my books with milk and graham crackers. But sometimes Kicki would read to me, and I'd nestle into her words, struck by the notion that this was what connected us—my mom, my aunts and uncle, my older cousins and younger—we had all been cradled by Kicki's stories. We had all been children in the crook of her arm. In the deep heat of summer, dazed from a nap, I'd listen to her voice glide across the pages, soft and cool like a cotton sheet. She would read from *The Shirley Temple Treasury*, a beautifully illustrated anthology my mother had loved as a little girl. I remember sitting on Kicki's lap on the upstairs porch, the city noises drifting through the rusted screen. A page of verdant mountains unfurled across her lap. She'd read me Shirley's "Heidi" until my eyes fluttered closed.

Fred, Kicki, the accident. All of these events had to happen, in the order they happened, at the intensity with which they happened, or my life as I know it would not be my life.

I emailed Mike. Then I waited for the snow to melt.

SUMMER

Chapter Six

I began my trip to Montauk in the rain.

It was the Thursday before Memorial Day, and I was about to leave my office in Rock Center. I'd spent the afternoon working on the marketing materials for a forthcoming book called *The Opposite of Loneliness* by Marina Keegan. It was the first project I had strongly advocated we acquire. Marina had graduated from Yale in 2012. She'd had a job lined up at the *New Yorker*, an apartment awaiting her in Brooklyn, and a serious boyfriend. Her laptop had contained a trove of essays and stories, some of which had won awards. Four days after graduation, on Memorial Day weekend, she had died in a car accident. She was twenty-two.

The Opposite of Loneliness, her first and last book, echoed with what could have been.

I thought about Marina as I exited the elevator. That weekend would mark the first anniversary of her death. In the lobby of the Simon & Schuster building, between gold deco moldings and marble columns, I said a little prayer to her.

The plan was to meet Mike and Shane at Fifty-Third and First at five thirty. They were some of the few people I knew who kept a car in the city—a hunter-green 2004 Land Rover Discovery with brush guards, a ladder, and tan leather interior. Shane diligently cared for it, adding washer fluid, Pennzoil, and premium gasoline. It was too much car for Manhattan, but it meshed with the tinctures of their glamorous relationship. They relished the chance to drive it out of town.

Over the past few months Mike had detailed the fees, rules, and scheduling of the share house. Each group email set off a cascade of inside jokes and references, an activation of shared history. It was clear that I had wandered into a self-contained world. The house was an ecosystem, complete with rituals, social structures, and systems of morality. I struggled to decipher it without context, but I had at least absorbed the house's name. It was called the Hive.

I'd chosen my dates with mounting anticipation. From Memorial Day to Labor Day there were sixteen weekends. Everyone was guaranteed eight. On the spreadsheet we ranked our preferences for the weekends in each month—one through four, marking an X next to any weekends with a known conflict. Then we ranked the holidays—Memorial Day, Fourth of July, and Labor Day—one through three. We were guaranteed at least two holiday weekends, and everyone was also entitled to two full weeks (ten weekdays) at the Hive. But those extended vacations had to be approved by the house leaders prior to the summer.

The other house leader was a financial analyst named Colby. Mike controlled the scheduling and Colby ran the books. They alone had access to the owner. As house leaders they were entitled to unlimited weekends and their choice of rooms, but if something went wrong, their names were on the lease. In early May they'd sent out a contract that each housemate had to return with a digital signature.

The Hive House Rules

Half Share
8 Weekends guaranteed
10 weekdays
Bed priority, unless an extremely crowded weekend

General House Information EVERYONE is to be familiar with:

- This is NOT a sharehouse; the term "sharehouse" is never to be used. Number of occupants is confidential. If any housemate implies anything to the contrary, there will be immediate consequences. As far as you're to be concerned, this is a house rented by a few couples whom you are visiting.
- No fraternizing with the neighbors. A hello and a smile is required, but no speaking to (the less contact the better)
- House address is _____. Know where it is and what it looks like. If anyone enters a neighbor's house by mistake there will be immediate consequences.
- Everyone is expected to pull their weight. Planning events, cleaning, cooking, calling cabs, knowing bouncers, food/alcohol errands, music/entertainment, etc. If you are asked to do something by a house captain, do it.
- House Captains: Mike, Colby

Overnight Guest policy

- Each person is allowed guests on any weekend, depending on house capacity
- Guests must be scheduled with house captains
- If guest is approved, price is $150 per guest per night
- Guests sleep with host, or on couch unless there is a bed available
- Full-cost must be paid to one of the house captains *prior* to guest arrival via cash, Paypal or check
- Guests are responsibility of housemate who brings them.

Room assignments

- Each weekend, you will have specific room and roommate assignments. You are required to stick to the room you were assigned. Couches may be used if there are no housemates reserved on them.

Cleaning

- *All housemates* are required to pick up after themselves, leave the house on Sunday in an acceptable manner. No matter what time you have to leave, you are required to contribute in some way.
- Professional cleaning service will do sheets, towels, and general cleaning each week (Mondays), but everyone has to chip in. We are paying by the hour. You must put your towels and sheets in the laundry room prior to departure.
- Each person must do laundry at least 2 of their weekends for the rest of the house. There will be a laundry chart and you can log in when you contribute so we can keep track of this.

Sexual Relations

- No sexual relations in any public area of the house (pool, living room, kitchen, etc.)
- No "Sexile"ing your roommates. (no locking doors for that matter)
- Zero tolerance for unwelcomed sexual advances. Respect your housemates, no is no.

Day Guests and Parties

- If guests are invited over during the day or for a party, this must be approved by house captains or by majority of housemates that weekend (not a free for all, be respectful)
- You are 100% responsible for the actions of your guests.
- Make sure your guests know our address and what the house looks like. If any of your guests enter/approach a neighbor's house by mistake there will be immediate consequences.

Supplies

- General house supplies will be stocked at the beginning of the summer. Extra supplies can be purchased out of the house account when needed, must be approved by house captains.

Calendar

- The calendar is set before summer begins (a week before Memorial day). All weekend requests/conflicts must be finalized before this date. Once the calendar is set, it is final. If you cannot make a weekend, you forfeit that weekend. Extenuating circumstances in which weekend swapping is requested is allowed and will be dealt with on a per case basis (just email house captains)

House Captain Benefits

- Since captain's names are on the lease and are liable, and did all the work to put the house together, they will get the following additional benefits:
- Extra weekends
- Top room picks

Noise violation

- Anyone present at the house and their guests will split any cost incurred.
- While we're not there to babysit each other, everyone should make a reasonable effort to keep other housemates in line if their behavior becomes a disruption to roommates or neighbors.

NO Fighting

- Absolutely no physical aggression or violence is permitted. Zero Tolerance, immediate eviction.
- No belligerence toward other housemates. If there are any problems or tension, bring it up with a house captain.

House budget

- The house budget was constructed using our experience from last summer. The house captains have included a sizeable safety buffer and budgeted generously. Should house costs exceed the planned budget and collected guest fees, all house-mates will be responsible for splitting the additional cost.

Other General Rules

- No Animals

- If you break something, you will pay for it in cash. Your security deposit does not automatically cover things you break.
- Do not take other peoples' food / towels / belongings without asking.
- Do not pour/throw things in the pool. You will pay for the extra cleaning.
- _Drinking and driving: zero tolerance policy. Automatic eviction_

Penalties for not abiding by rules

- First offence is $200 fine paid to the house pot.
- Second offence is a loss of a weekend and additional $200 fine.
- Third offence is eviction.

I,

_____,
agree to the rules above and understand the repercussions if I do not adhere to them.

Signature _____

Date:

_____

Most of the clauses seemed prudent, but the idea of inciting a fine was mortifying. I wondered if these rules were informed by past fiascos. What sort of crazy shit had gone down the summer before?

A cold mist slicked the glass buildings on Sixth Avenue, the beads slowly gathering to a downpour. By the time I reached the corner of Fifty-Third and First, I was drenched. The Land Rover was live-parked by a McDonald's.

I tossed my duffel bag in the trunk and jumped in the back. Shane was in the driver's seat and Mike sat shotgun. Kirsten, Mike's best friend from childhood, moved over to make room for me. She had visited Mike at college and I'd known her since freshman year.

"OMG, you're soaked to the bone!"

Kirsten's eyes were big and expressive, a bewitched green. Her beauty was hard to take in. Long blond hair framing a heart-shaped face, a quiet symmetry. She was mellow, an observer, but always friendly.

"Do you know Colby?" she asked.

He was leaning against the window, his pressed shirt loose at the collar.

"Hi!" he said, extending his hand. "I'm your Hive dad!"

I recognized him from Mike's social media. His hair was gelled and slicked back. A laptop case sat by his feet. He'd begged off his desk Friday by vowing to log in remotely.

"Can you believe it? Memorial Day weekend and they got me workin'. Let a girl live!"

Mike had cracked the window and was smoking a cigarette.

"Will you put that thing out?" Shane chided. "You're letting in the rain."

"Oh, come on. It's just water."

"I got the car detailed yesterday. You can smoke when the rain stops. Put it out."

Shane fiddled with his iPhone's radio adapter and pressed play on Klingande's "Jubel," a tropical house song that felt like summer. He pulled into the slow crawl of traffic, the cones of headlights. Aqueous shadows roved across the dash. We were off.

As night fell, the rain ceased and traffic began to fade away.
Shane juiced the speed. We were energized by the sensation of
actually driving, but the slick roads beneath us jolted me back
to winter and the car accident. Those stop-motion scenes—the
skidding and sliding, the way the wheel locked up, the violent
somersault, the shatter of glass—were never far away. I was here,
I reminded myself, because of Kicki.

I kept these thoughts to myself, and as the conversation mo-
tored about freely, I mostly listened. Kirsten and Colby were un-
guarded, and I relaxed into the exchange. They talked about past
hookups, drunken escapades, the places in the city where they'd
left their credit cards, and I chimed in here and there. Colby was,
in his words, "single and hungry." Kirsten was single, too.

"Everyone finds love in Montauk," Kirsten said. "Even if it's
just for the night."

In Manorville, we pulled into a Cumberland Farms for beer,
chips, and jerky. Shane filled the gas tank. The parking lot over-
flowed with luxury cars glistening beneath a fluorescent over-
hang. The air savored of gasoline and wet pavement.

"Everyone who's anyone is at this Cumberland Farms on a
Friday," said Colby. I couldn't tell if he was joking.

Over seventy miles in, Long Island split into two forks. To the
north lay vineyards, antiques shops, flowerbox beach towns. To
the south: the Hamptons. It barely made sense to me that Long
Island could contain Brooklyn and Queens, let alone two elusive
eastern prongs. At the farthest tip of the South Fork, at the very
end of the Hamptons, Montauk speared the Atlantic like a long-
armed fist, earning the nickname The End.

As the beers flowed in the back seat, I learned more about my housemates. A daunting thirty-one people had signed on for half shares. All but a handful were second-year veterans. Most housemates fell into one of three buckets: the girls, the finance guys, and the gays.

"I'm in two buckets," Colby said. "Got my finance bros and my gays." He turned to me. "You're in a bucket of your own."

Colby had first gone to Montauk two summers prior. He'd barely had time to drop off his bags before his boyfriend—a guy eight years his senior—whisked him into town. They took shots at the Point, then hit the dance floor of the Memory Motel until four a.m. The next morning they woke up and drank mudslides at the Royal Atlantic Hotel. Then they dozed on the beach until it was time to do it all again. A couple weeks later Colby broke up with the guy, but he'd fallen in love with Montauk. He met Mike that autumn and the house took shape.

"For me it was different," said Mike. "I've been going out to Montauk since I was a kid. Two weeks every August. First time I drank was at a beach bonfire in Montauk."

We rode through Southampton and into Bridgehampton, passing fields lined with shuttered fruit stands. In East Hampton, we drove down Further Lane, a street that lent its name to a hedge fund. The back roads were narrow and hemmed by topiary, leaving much of the landscape to the imagination. On certain streets the front lawns opened up, revealing clapboard estates and driveways made of crushed seashells.

East Hampton's town center felt like a suburban extension of Fifth Avenue. Sotheby's, J.Crew, Ralph Lauren, Dylan's Candy

Bar. The pharmacy was called an apothecary. A movie theater boasted an old-time marquee. It was nothing like the honky-tonk beaches I'd known as a child, where bikers revved their hogs in pizza-joint parking lots.

Where our family vacationed, you had to bring everything. Coleman coolers packed with Hi-C juice boxes, cans of Del Monte pears and Chef Boyardee. For a week away my great-aunt Annie once brought a washing machine and dryer. It was that kind of beach and we were that kind of family.

By Amagansett, the last town before Montauk, the trees grew taller. Trappings of the Hamptons still lingered—surf boutiques, upscale taquerias, gilded verandas—but the money-clipped strictures began to slacken.

"Look!" Kirsten called. "There's Talkhouse!" On the left side of the road stood a cobbled warren of strobe-lit dance rooms, a sign that read STEPHEN TALKHOUSE.

"It's the craziest bar ever," she said. "We go there on Fridays sometimes. It's a bit of a hike from Montauk, so you have to commit, but it's worth it. They bring in an eighties cover band that plays in the city. You always bump into someone you know."

"It's definitely the most fun bar in Amagansett," added Colby. "The line is out of control but we just cut it because of Ashley."

"Yeah, Ashley's obsessed with Talkhouse," Kirsten continued. "She goes prepared. She once left her hair straightener there and went back in the morning to get it."

"Who's Ashley?" I asked.

"She's my roommate in the city," Kirsten said. "She's from Fairfield. She's…"

"She's the Mayor of Montauk," Mike finished. "You'll meet her soon enough."

At the border of Amagansett and Montauk, Shane opened the moonroof, letting in the stars. Outside I sensed a sand-blasting, a peeling away. We had driven past the point of civilization into a wild, moon-dipped isthmus. The air whipped cold and pungent through our open windows. I could see the ocean on both sides. Beyond the sand banks stood sleek, streamlined houses with flat roofs.

We passed three fish shacks—Lunch, Clam Bar, and Cyril's— the last channel markers before Montauk. After Cyril's the highway split. We continued down the Old Montauk Highway. Beyond the occasional fire hydrant and the dip of telephone poles, the road was stripped of human interference. We wove between tangled pines on one side and diving views of the ocean on the other.

The street names in Montauk were written vertically on white stakes, and they shined like thin ghosts in the headlights. We turned onto our street in Hither Hills and curved up a narrow road. As Shane flipped on the blinker, I tapped into the night's star-washed energy. A wood-beamed house appeared on a hill. We had reached the Hive.

Chapter Seven

My first night at the Hive shimmered with a low-key radiance. We were tired from the drive and slipped into sweatshirts. Mike turned on the TV, just to have something playing in the background. *Hook* was on TBS. The others weren't scheduled to arrive until the next day.

We drank rosé and slid back into our conversation. Colby told us about his job and how stressed he'd been lately. He worked as an analyst in fixed income; I had no idea what that meant, but I sensed a darker concern embroidered within his words, a holding back. One minute he seemed engaged and amiable; the next he got lost in a somber daze. Colby was flamboyant but not effeminate, and his "gayness" seemed to toggle on and off. He existed on multiple planes at once.

Kirsten was a style editor at Ralph Lauren and liked her job fine. Her bigger problem was relationships. She kept going after the wrong guys.

Mike told us about the Montauk of his youth. The Sloppy Tuna bar used to be Nick's. Montauk Beach House used to be Ronjo. Surf Lodge was Lakeside. As a kid he used to go to Montauk with his extended family every August. Then his uncle Tim died in the Twin Towers on 9/11. Montauk was the same until it wasn't.

Hook ended and Mike fiddled with the remote. The television was stuck on the channel guide and wouldn't refresh. I got up and attempted to change it manually, to no avail. The cable box and channel guide both read 11:11, but our phones said it was 11:14. The TV had also frozen on 11:11. It stayed like that for the rest of the night.

We took the frozen TV as a portent of our arrival. Mike claimed the number 11 followed him wherever he went, though its meaning to him was unclear. The Hive was said to be haunted, and I'd eventually hear all the stories. But I held to the adage that 11:11 brought luck. You could hang your hopes on that number, make a wish. Perhaps it would come true.

I was assigned to a room in the basement, but stayed that night in an empty upstairs bedroom. As I settled in, I experienced an inner stirring. The car accident, those months before, had reduced me to a larval state. But now I felt myself reaching for more.

Sleep came quickly that night—thick and dreamless, a harkening back to my first night of college. As with the Hive, BC and its pinwheel of unfamiliar senses wore me out on the first day. After a barbecue in the quad and some pilfered vodka shots in a dorm room I fell asleep instantly. My mom had washed my extra-long twin sheets to make them smell like home.

My real struggle had come the night before, as I attempted to fall asleep for the last time in my childhood bed. I remember the blue light through the window, the glow of my Moonbeam alarm clock. The basketball, skiing, and tennis trophies on my bookcase. The collage of photos and magazine clippings I'd decoupaged to my wall—an evolving expression of my half-formed inner life. The air conditioner hummed, but summer was over. I would wake up in the morning and my life would be drastically different. I would never again live permanently with my parents. I didn't know who I was or what I would become. And even though it wasn't the case, not by a long shot, I was, to my young mind, on my own.

I awoke the next morning in the same position I had fallen asleep in, buried beneath a white chenille blanket. I felt refreshed in a way I hadn't in months.

The bedroom was small and cozy with wood veneer furniture and its own private balcony. I sleepily stepped onto the deck. It had rained in the night and the planks were damp. The Hive was situated in a heavily wooded area, and two red birds flapped through a tall pine tree that stood close by. I hadn't noticed the tree the night before, but now I could see the rain droplets clinging to its waxy needles.

Red birds, my aunt Ellen said, were signs of the departed. They appeared when we needed them, to remind us we were not alone. In our family, a cardinal meant Kicki. I thought about her final days. How our entire extended family gathered at the hospital to be near her. Kicki's sister Annie made the trip up from Southington, Connecticut, and held her hand. Annie could always make her laugh.

As Kicki was staring into Annie's eyes, she made a confession. *I miss my mom.* It felt like a private thought, something she hadn't meant to articulate out loud. *I miss my mom.* Her mother had died decades ago. Kicki was ninety-two. And she still missed her mom.

When it was clear the end was approaching, my dad, who was her primary care physician, asked her if she would like to go home, to her own bed. *That would be lovely, dear,* she said.

I felt Kicki's presence as I stepped out of the bedroom. I was the first one awake. I began to explore.

The Hive had two other upstairs bedrooms, the master (aka Princess Room) and Mike and Shane's room. I peered into the Princess Room, where Colby and Kirsten were still sleeping. The room had cathedral ceilings, exposed rafters, and a wall of closets with mirrored doors. One of those doors stood open, revealing a pink flower-stitched kimono on a plastic hanger. It couldn't have belonged to Kirsten. Maybe Colby, but doubtful. I assumed it was the owner's, something she kept in Montauk year-round. You never know when you might need a pink flower-stitched kimono.

Mike and Shane were also asleep, tethered together on a narrow, low-slung futon. Their room was small and beachy, a sloping alcove. An oil painting of a sailboat hung above their nicked dresser. I imagined Mike had already loaded its drawers with his summer clothes—Lacoste shirts, Vilebrequin bathing suit, running shorts and pants from Vineyard Vines.

I went downstairs. The living room, like the rest of the house, had pine paneling of an older vintage and a maroon shag carpet, which I was surprised to learn had replaced the previous year's *white* shag carpet. Every wall and ceiling in the house was made of unlacquered tongue-and- groove wood. Trapped within them were the scents of salt, must, and firewood. Kirsten had described it as a seventies porn den. I thought of it as *On Golden Pond* with a dash of *The Shining*.

I ran my hands across the old records on the built-in bookshelf: the Beach Boys, Herman's Hermits, Carole King. Magazines from the seventies (how they'd survived in such pristine condition we'd never know) fanned the wicker side tables. To the right was a bay window and beneath that a banquette with mismatched accent pillows packed so densely they stood vertical. A second bookshelf contained wondrously random books. *A Field Guide to Birds' Nests in the United States East of the Mississippi River. Little Dorrit.* A Viking edition of *The Portable Nietzsche.* Many of them didn't have jackets. I inspected a copy of *The Communist Manifesto*, its salt-cracked spine bent with humidity.

The kitchen and dining room were separated by a Formica island lined with jars, mixing bowls, and the empty remains of our thirty-pack. I pushed aside the cream-colored drapes to let in the light. The kitchen opened to a screened-in porch and a deck that cantilevered a steep, tree-lined hill. At the bottom of the hill was the swimming pool.

I walked out to the deck. It was an overcast day and the clouds hung like gourds. The exterior of the house, like the inside, was framed with wooden clapboards. I admired the rising latticework of decks, railings, and stairs, the oddly shaped roof that looked like a honeycomb.

Our Hither Hills neighborhood was wedged between two parallel highways—the Old Montauk Highway and the New Montauk Highway—which weren't highways really, just beach roads with high speed limits. All the houses seemed woodsy and secluded, perching on twisty roads that only Mike could name. He knew this place down to its marrow. But Montauk was no longer the Shangri-la of his youth. Loss, as he had told us the night before, had rendered it complex. Still, something had compelled him to return.

To me Montauk was still a blank space. In the months before the ground thawed, it had served as my fulcrum. On wind-battered nights in March and April I'd go to the gym and stare at my reflection. Over bicep curls and leg lifts I'd mentally track the weeks until Memorial Day. *Seven weeks*, I'd tell myself as sweat ribboned down my arms. *Six weeks now. Five. Something will change. Something will open up. You just need to make it till then.*

The song in my earbuds would end, and I'd hear the rusty creak of the gym's weight machines. The basement facility had the no-frills air of a Philadelphia boxing ring. For an hour and a half each night I descended, head down, into its concrete depths, lifting weights next to men double my size. I punished my body in those workouts, pushing myself beyond the threshold of physical strain to a place where thought evaporated. I wrenched my neck multiple times that winter for no reason. I hurt my elbow. I didn't know why I was doing this. I just knew I needed to.

After the gym I'd go to the supermarket, where I'd buy prepared food from the deli counter. I'd return home and eat my grilled chicken or breaded fish in front of the television, then immediately get ready for bed. My roommates were spending more nights with their girlfriends. On the nights they stayed, I felt better. It was a comfort just knowing I wasn't in the apartment alone. But when they were both gone, I felt the full weight of my thoughts. A dark hand pressing onto my chest. To self-soothe, I thought about Montauk.

Around noon it started to rain. I changed into a sweatshirt and joined the others in Shane's car. We drove to the Bridgehampton Kmart. Navigating the lacquered aisles, we filled two carts with paper towels, laundry detergent, toothpaste, hand soap, twenty-packs of toilet paper, bottles of No-Ad sunscreen, bug spray, seltzer water, jars of peanut butter, and two-packs of Pantene Pro-V shampoo.

Shane liked to drive through the rich neighborhoods. On the way home he showed us the Duke family mansion: "See those dark cedar shingles? Those are distinct to the Hamptons. You don't see those on the Cape or Islands." We drove by Ralph Lauren's house and the Andy Warhol estate. Shane worked in finance but had an eye for design. He knew how to curate. In Mike's dorm-like apartment in Stuytown, Shane had installed an oriental carpet, a mahogany boudoir, chinoiserie bowls, and a vase of calla lilies, the trash bins filling with Mike's Disney posters and Office Max desk lamps.

We got back to the Hive and were unloading the supplies in the kitchen when the first car arrived. Colby shut the cabinet and spun around, his fingers dancing. "Now y'all be on your best behavior," he declared in a faux southern accent. "Mama's got eighteen more babies coming tonight. Mama's got *com*pany."

I checked my reflection in the tiki-framed mirror. My hair was askew. I tried to smooth it down. I only knew one other housemate who was coming out that weekend: my coworker Perrie. We'd become close, but we'd never spent time together outside the office. I wondered how our two spheres might merge.

The others moved to the living room. I trailed. I told myself to relax. Chill. Be cool.

Two guys climbed out of a royal-blue Audi. They wore high-seamed shorts, leather Sperrys, and T-shirts that clung to their arms. Even their duffel bags looked fashionable.

The shorter of the two skylarked into the living room. He removed his aviators and glared from wall to wall with discerning familiarity.

"The lesbian painting's still on the wall. And there's the shitty couch that everyone has sex on. Oh my God wait they got a *new* shag carpet?" He hugged Kirsten. "Hi, baby. Your hair smells good. Shane, did you already take an ax to the wicker cabinet? Someone get me a drink."

"It must be summer again. Timmy's color-blocking," Kirsten said, grabbing him by the T-shirt.

Timmy's bag hit the floor with a thud. "Where's Ashley? Is she here yet? I need her energy."

"No Ashley this weekend," Mike said.

"Stop."

"She's studying for the CFA."

"Wait. Seriously. Where is she?"

"I *am* serious!"

"She just got back from a work trip in Vegas," Kirsten added.

"Stop. I can't." He turned to me and held out his hand. "Hi, so rude of me, I'm Timmy."

"Hi. I'm John. Nice to meet you."

"Mike's BC friend, right? Welcome to the Hive."

"Thanks."

"Are you gay or straight?"

"Haha, what!"

"Where are you sleeping?"

"Umm...the Game Room?"

"Straight." His attention turned to the kitchen. "Look at all those vodka handles. Do you know the ABCD's of the Hive?"

I noticed the other housemate standing silently at the threshold. He was scanning the room dizzily, one leg pretzeled around the other, his neon Nikes hugging. He looked like a Jane Austen character: night-black hair, ice-chipped eyes, freckled skin. Narrow nose. Narrow cheeks. Wiry, with veins running down his biceps.

"What are the ABCD's?" I asked.

"Alcohol, Booze, Chips, and Dick."

There was an airiness about the other housemate. He reminded me of Peter Pan. He glanced around eagerly, smiling at Timmy's histrionics. I noticed how he kept spinning his watch around his wrist—a small tell, a percolation of manic energy. I could sense his urgent need to size up the room.

We caught eyes. A split-second determination, a recognition, a mutual unlocking, an alignment. I could tell from his bewildered amusement that we were thinking the same thing. *I don't know what I just walked into, but I guess I'm about to find out.*

"Hi," he said. "I'm Matt."

Chapter Eight

People began to show up. From anywhere in the house you could hear them, the judder of the sliding door, the thunk of a duffel, a pronouncement of arrival. *Hello! We're back! The Hive!* Each arrival brought a jolt of fresh energy, an addictive sense of accrual. I pictured those paint-by-numbers books, the colors filling in slowly, then seemingly all at once.

Who would walk through the door next? Who was still on the road? It was reported that the Long Island Expressway was a parking lot. Route 27 was worse. An hour to drive through Amagansett alone. The four thirty "Cannonball" train from Penn Station was standing room only for the first two hours, tallboy beer cans, crushed and empty, tossed across the piss-covered bathrooms. No one had ever seen such crowds.

Mike instructed me to shower upstairs, quickly, because hot water was scarce. I grabbed a towel from the linen closet and closed the door but did not lock it, fearing it impolite. The bathroom had a blue inlay tub with frosted glass sliders that afforded at least some modicum of privacy. I turned the clear plastic spigot until the water grew tolerable, the room filling with steam. Last summer's sand clung to the strips of tack beneath my feet. I showered as fast as I could.

I got out and toweled off. In the mirror I polished away a circle of condensation, revealing my brown eyes, my freckled nose, my damp blond hair. A fresh wave of loneliness washed over me. More housemates arriving. I could hear them.

I attempted to pump myself up. *You're great. You're fun. People love you. This is a new adventure. This is exciting. You look good.*

The voice in my head was my mom's.

I sought my dad for practical concerns, but my mother was my soothsayer. When I was stressed, overwhelmed, or emotionally deflated, I'd call her to comfort me. The mere sound of her voice—steady, smooth, and luminous—made me feel better. She always knew the right thing to say.

Back home she kept a small drawer of treasures. A gilded set of prayer-worn rosary beads, a Miraculous Medal, and a silver pendant of a synchronized swimmer in a cobalt-blue bathing suit and bathing cap. The pendant was the size of a fingernail and had survived many moves. My mom won it at the New England synchronized swimming championships in 1964 with a solo routine to Arthur Fiedler's "Sleigh Ride." Her sisters and she were members of the local parish team, the Holy Name Aqualinas. The noncompetitive team, which practiced in the same pool, was called the Dolphinettes. Both teams were coached by Helena Waddlegger. These names were like wood beams in our family's mythic pantheon.

When I was growing up my mom rarely swam, but when she did the water transformed her. She became magnetic. Elemental. I remember one night at the public pool. It must've been mid-July or early August, when the day's heat seemed to collect in the evening trill of cicadas. My mom dove in and I watched, mesmerized, as the water slicked back her hair. I let go from the lap lane and swam toward her. The sky had gone dark and the pool was illuminated by spotlights. She swanned through the water and we floated together, laughing. Then she did her tricks and tried to teach me. The ballet leg. The dolphin. The kip. I wrapped my arms around her neck and let her ferry me through the pool, its surface a mosaic of shattering white gold. We were the only two, swimming beneath the spotlights.

I remember the pressing need to be near her, to not let go.

Alone in the musty Game Room, I considered various outfits before settling on a lightweight cardigan and jeans. My bag, which I'd arranged on the cold damp futon, looked like an exploded spring roll. I styled my hair with paste. I smoothed my cheeks with store-brand lotion. I rolled up my sleeves, rolled them back down. Took off the sweater entirely. Did I look okay? Would these people like me?

Everyone seemed outgoing, though I'd quickly detected the translucent divides. There were two tribes of girls: the immaculately dressed D.Lo, Perrie, Kirsten, and Dana, and the more laid-back Kara, Carolyn, and Taylor. The gay guys: Mike, Shane, Colby, Tyler, and Timmy, who moved between the girls and the gregarious finance bros: Bradley, Johnson, and Arthur. Then a few others, like Matt and me, who were either new or floated.

It was, of course, a privileged milieu. Most of the housemates hailed from the tristate area and held degrees from top-tier schools. Not everyone had money, but everyone had access. Everyone lived in Manhattan. Everyone had a career path. Everyone seemed to have a gym membership at Equinox.

In this cocoon of fortune our perspectives flattened. All of our problems existed in one dimension. Minor vexation and true hardship were one and the same. Small annoyances—an unanswered text, a sold-out SoulCycle class, a crippling hangover—rendered us inert. A Starbucks drink made incorrectly was a personal attack.

There was no distinguishing between drama and melodrama that summer. It was all part of the story, and I needed to grasp what that meant if I wanted to fit in.

From the landing I could smell the burnt clamps of hair straighteners, the acerbic cut of hair spray. I passed by bedrooms aswarm with totes. The furious purr of inflating air mattresses.

One by one people gathered in the kitchen until everyone was there. Colby put on "The Way You Make Me Feel" by Michael Jackson. It was one of my favorite songs, triggering memories of a dance party I threw in high school one night when my parents went out to dinner.

Across the counter a menagerie of chip bags were splayed open: Doritos, SunChips, Ruffles, Cape Cod, BBQ, Sour Cream and Onion. Jars of ranch dip, artichoke spread, and mango salsa pocked the kitchen island like small aboveground pools. Since Memorial Day was a special occasion, Colby ordered four cheese pizzas on the house account. The pizza boxes were stacked across the stove. I devoured two slices in the corner.

Ice cubes cracked under streams of Smirnoff vodka. The girls were fixing their drinks at the same time. They were dressed in form-fitting bandage dresses, wedges, silk garments I'd later learn were called rompers, all of them glowing, the gray malaise of the city scrubbed off them.

The finance bros were loud and drunk. They kept going from the basement back to the kitchen. Arthur appeared to be their den mother. He was big, broad and tall enough to change a light bulb on flat feet. He'd grown up in Chappaqua and lived with three other guys in a bro pad on Fourteenth Street. He entered this and every summer with no agenda other than to make friends, drink beer, grill food, and have fun. He wrapped his hairy arm around me like a mother bear pulling in her cub. I was up next for beer pong. Who was my partner?

I scanned the room. Neither Mike nor Shane was big on drinking games, and Kirsten and Perrie were still getting ready upstairs.

I glanced at Matt, who was standing by the breezeway. He was locked in conversation with D.Lo, his Solo cup resting in the crook of his elbow. He turned around. The empty cups on the table signaled a finished game.

"Hey." He nodded. "Do you need a partner?"

He moved through the room with light, carefree steps, eyes darting. His shoulders were square and straight as a coat hanger. He looked both boyish and world-weary. Anxious but confident. I had never seen anyone quite like him.

We filled up the cups, reaching for the Ping-Pong balls at the same time. Our hands touched, and we smiled at each other. I realized we were the exact same height.

"Are you good?" he asked.

"Good?" The simple question threw me. "I mean, I try to be? I don't jaywalk."

He laughed. "I'm talking about the game."

I grew crimson. Of course he was talking about the game. "Oh yeah, I guess I'm decent. Are you?"

"I go on streaks depending on who I play with. We'll either win big or lose terribly. But it's always the same."

"I have a feeling we'll be good," I said.

"I do too."

I finished filling our cups.

"You shoot first," he said.

We won our first game, then our second. Matt claimed he played better with a buzz. We poured celebratory shots of tequila from a long blue bottle and grimaced as we kicked them back without limes.

"Where I grew up in Virginia they called it beer pong, not Beirut," he said. "But then I got to college and people called it both."

The tequila was warming my chest, pinning me to the moment. Colby was readjusting his nautical belt and button-down in the mirror. Perrie was glued to her phone. On the other side of the table Kirsten rinsed off one of the Ping-Pong balls in a cup of water. She kept looking up at Matt and me.

"It was interchangeable for us, too," I said. "At least flip cup is flip cup."

"I love flip cup."

"So do I."

"Let's play it next," he said, then, tapping a finger between us, "Same team."

The house cups were soft plastic and translucent, sturdy enough to withstand the dishwasher but cheap enough to be left in a cab. They were monogrammed with THE HIVE 2013 and embossed with a honeybee. I noticed stacks of them in a plastic sleeve beneath a chair.

"These cups are so cute," Matt said. "I wanna steal a few for my apartment."

I handed him one. "You totally should."

"Would people get mad?"

"Not if they don't find out."

"Cover for me." He tucked a loose cup in a freestanding drawer.

"Remind me it's there."

He touched my forearm and I flinched, I wasn't sure why.

There was a commotion in the living room. Someone paused the music. Timmy barreled around the kitchen island, his glass of white wine catching bars of light.

"No. Stop. Get out."

A statuesque blonde clutching an electronic BMW key entered hair-first. Her skin was tan and her teeth were white. She wore a white tank top and cut-off jeans. My first thought was that she resembled a Barbie doll. Narrow waist, long legs, feet angled into heels. Her eyes were big and green and studded with fake eyelashes that opened and closed like butterflies. She carried an overstuffed pink pearlized bag. I could easily picture her at a thatched bar in Cancún, nursing a neon pink drink. This was Ashley.

She momentarily short-circuited my brain. The symmetry of

her face; her flat, tan stomach; the way her breasts seemed to defy gravity. She spoke breathlessly, addressing everyone.

"Guys, I was just in the city and was like, what am I doing, why am I not in Montauk, I needed to be with my loves. I love you all so much I just couldn't not be here!"

She tossed a fat yellow CFA study guide across the counter. It landed next to a pack of Philadelphia cream cheese that had been partitioned by Tostitos. I'd heard about the prestigious credential, chartered financial analyst, and the rigorous three-part exam one had to pass to earn it. The process could take four years or more.

"But like, I have to study. I'm going to fail. What time is it? I just got back from Vegas. I'm not even going to shower, I'm wearing this out, I don't even care." She glanced dismissively at her white tank top and ripped jean shorts. "I'm just going to get ready real quick. Oh my God you guys, you all look so amazing, like seriously you all look like models. Taylor, you look stunning in that dress."

She approached Kirsten and grabbed her by the shoulder.

"Thank you for keeping it a surprise, roomie," she said, looking her up and down. "Ugh. You just look so beautiful."

Ashley worked in the finance department of a boutique real estate firm. That week her company had hosted an event at the Bellagio. At night the fountains surged and danced, and Ashley watched them alone from her window. The firm held its daily meetings at a poolside cabana. Ashley extolled market analysis in a pink bikini.

She grabbed the vodka and began to pour with both hands. I was standing next to her and could smell the floral scent of her hair product.

She finished pouring and looked up. "I know you."

Her voice was caramel-dipped. It took me a moment to register that she was addressing me.

"Hi. I'm John. Mike's friend from BC."

"I've seen you in Mike's pictures. And you're Matt, right? I'm Ashley."

Matt and I both stared in confused wonder.

She turned back to me. "I hear you're a writer and, like, the funniest person in the house."

I told her I was a book editor, but that I wrote a little on the side. And I didn't know if I was funny.

"I need to read more. I'm such a numbers person. Look, I just need to straighten my hair real quick, and then I'll be ready to go out with you guys."

You guys. I remember this. For a second, for Ashley, no one else in the house existed but the three of us.

She returned ten minutes later in an ocean-gray bandage dress. Her hair was somehow even straighter. It shimmered a luminous dirty-blond. She looked like Britney Spears circa "Toxic." She looked like a pageant contestant.

"Cab's here in ten minutes!" someone shouted.

Ashley sat on a stool and opened her CFA book. Someone handed her a shot of tequila. On the other side of the island, Carolyn and Taylor were dancing. Others circled the table for flip cup. A phone camera flashed as Perrie and Bonnie angled for a selfie.

"Under which measurement scale is data categorized, but not ranked? A, an ordinal scale; B, a nominal scale; C, an interval scale...B, a nominal scale."

Ashley flipped to an answer key, nodded, and returned to the initial page.

Mike handed her another shot of tequila. She downed it.

"The joint probability of events *A* and *B* is thirty-two percent with the probability of event *A* being sixty percent and the—"

"Wait, sorry." Matt tapped her on the shoulder. "Are you studying for the CFA right now? While pregaming?"

"I take the test next week and I hear it's super hard."

She reached for the tequila.

"A company has just issued five million dollars of mandatory redeemable preferred shares with a par value of one hundred dollars per share and a seven percent..."

Montauk had many cab companies, but we always used Montauk's Best Taxi. The driver, Henry, was friends with all the returnees. He spent his winters in Colombia and his summers in Montauk, and seemed to own only tank tops. He was tan, a gym buff, short and muscled.

"Dana, my *girrrrl!*" he shouted through the window. "My bees are back in da *Hiiiiive.*"

The entire house piled into his massive yellow van. It had leather seats like a school bus and a back floor that could fit a handful of people willing to endure the road bumps. Ashley brought her CFA book and read by the light of her phone.

As we whirred along the Old Montauk Highway, Robyn's "Dancing On My Own" blared out the open front windows. Henry toggled the light switch to the beat of the song, transforming the cab into a disco. Squished in the back, I leaned my head against the windowpane, a cold gust rippling my shirt. Everyone was singing along, racing to finish their drinks before we reached town. With each ebb of the road my stomach dropped. I couldn't see the ocean, but I could tell it was there, far below.

Henry pulled up to the Memory Motel. It was a long, flat motel with twelve rooms and a parking lot facing the street, which had been emptied of vehicles and fenced in to become an outdoor bar. On the left side of the building an indoor bar with saloon-style double doors echoed music. I watched people moving in and out.

The Memory Motel. The Mem for short. The Rolling Stones wrote a song about it. Andy Warhol had often popped in. The Mem was a Montauk fixture, a backdrop of chaos. A flexion point in the night when memory itself began to fade.

"The Mem is crazy," said D.Lo. "Colby saw my ex here last summer and dumped a beer on his head."

"I lost my cell phone, money clips, and five credit cards here. In August alone." added Shane.

"Once at the Mem I got hit in the face with a sheet cake," said Kirsten.

The rooms were façaded with chipped white paint and a forest-green trim. Technically you could stay there, but no one we knew really did. The main draw was the bar, a red neon dive with a small stage, Hoop Fever, and Bud Light in aluminum bottles. We got out of the cab and ditched our cups in a bush. A line, fifty-deep, snaked along the sidewalk.

Each weekend in Montauk had a rhythm unveiled only in hindsight. Weather, weddings, and holidays played a part, but you could never tell beforehand whether the weekend would be quiet or busy. Fridays differed from Saturdays. Lines varied night to night, bar to bar. Sometimes a queue would move lightning quick. Other times you'd wait so long you'd get sober.

"Guys, these crowds are insane," said Kirsten.

"It's gonna be like this all summer," said Tyler. "Hurricane Sandy's flushed all the Jersey Shore crowd up here." In our limited interactions, Tyler struck me as one of the more levelheaded housemates. Circumspect and unflappable, he seemed to balance out the Hive's larger personalities. If he said the crowds would be bad, I believed him.

Another group our size stumbled out of a bright pink van. They walked straight up to the front of the line, all waving wads of cash. The bouncer instantly lashed them away.

Colby patted down his hair. "Nuh-uh, we are not waitin' in this line. Ashley, girl, come up here."

Ashley stood arms akimbo, piercing the crowd. "My guy isn't here. I don't see him."

"Girl, make a new guy."

"How many in our group? Fifteen?"

"Eighteen."

I watched as she made her approach, framed by a cone of light, the mica-mixed sidewalk sparkling beneath her. She directed the bouncer's attention toward our group, loosely touched his arm. I tried to look cool. To look like someone who belonged on the other side of the white dividing rope.

The bouncer wavered for a minute before dipping his chin. The others acted nonchalant as we flooded the entrance. I tried my best to mimic them, to walk slow, to keep my chin up high, to appear indifferent. But inside I was swelling with a giddy rush. For the first time in a long time, I felt popular. I felt part of something. We had just cut a line of fifty people. This, I learned, was the Hive.

Chapter Nine

The next morning, the house was still and gray. Rain pattered the slanting roofs, the piled decks and staircases. I was still asleep downstairs as blue light filtered through the blinds of the living room and into Kirsten's eyes.

She had fallen asleep on the couch next to Stefano. They both worked in fashion, in creative roles. He was twelve years older than she was, with a salt-and-pepper beard and silver hair that jungled across his forehead like layers of banana leaf. His eyes were intelligent and mischievous. They matched the clouds that broke through the window. His hand was rising and falling over his hairy chest.

Kirsten grew up on the Connecticut shore. As a kid she could walk out her front door and jump into the sand. In her Little Mermaid bathing suit she plucked snails from tide stones. She washed her feet with the hose so she wouldn't track sand into the house. She was shy and bookish. She spent hours in bed reading Lucy Maud Montgomery and the poetry of e. e. cummings, losing herself in their tangles of language.

In eighth grade, when her looks changed, girls who had ridiculed her in elementary school began to seek her friendship. She had always wanted to be good-looking, and the attention she received from her male classmates boosted her confidence. But inside she was still the girl who curled up with *Anne of Green Gables*. She still felt like no one could see her.

In college Kirsten developed an eating disorder. Pretty girls seemed to like her because she was pretty, but her inner and outer selves were out of alignment. She felt like two half-formed people. It took therapy and depression medication to wrest back control of her life.

After college Hurricane Sandy pummeled the Connecticut shore, and Kirsten's parents' home was destroyed. Eight months later, her parents were still displaced. Kirsten's mother had begun to rely on her for emotional support. The Hive became Kirsten's anchor that summer. Her port of call.

The last time she had hooked up with Stefano had been in March. He wasn't interested in a relationship, but they had continued to spend time together as friends. Kirsten's spring darkened under the pain of these encounters. Each one sharpened her longing. She thought if they kept seeing each other, he'd change his mind.

As the rain drummed the deck, she reached for her glass of water. Next to it, on the coffee table, were Stefano's tortoiseshell sunglasses. He had gone straight from happy hour to the bar without changing.

Stefano blinked awake, eyes rimmed with panic. For a second he did not know where he was. Kirsten gave him a sip of her water, and he tugged at her sweatshirt.

"I've missed you," he said, and pulled her head against his chest. For the first time since arriving in Montauk, she exhaled.

I went for a run, early, before full light. The streets were slick and blanketed in fog, and when my earbuds fell out from sweat, I could hear the birds. I'd set off with no particular route, just planned to run fifteen minutes out and fifteen minutes back. In the city, I liked to run along the West Side Highway, framed by the tall buildings, river jetties, and views of the Statue of Liberty. Running was how I acclimated. No matter how lonely and out of place I felt, running gave me a sense of ownership.

My legs ached. My lungs burned. I could smell the vodka seeping into my shirt. A big blue stamp tattooed my inner wrist. The word *OK* in a circle.

Okay. Okay. You're doing this. Okay.

I thought back to the night before, the clustered dancing and shots of Fireball from small plastic condiment cups. The bar was illuminated by neon signs and the music echoed through a blast of drunken yells. At one point I went to the parking lot while Ashley smoked a Parliament. She asked me why I was single and I said I didn't know. Then Matt dithered toward us, his gaze off kilter, his hair damp with sweat. He winged his arms across my shoulders. When Matt was drunk his affectations shined through. His wrists softened, shoulders narrowed, neck hunched.

Ashley stamped out her cigarette. She looked at the two of

us, wrapped arm-in-arm. Her lips parted, about to speak, then closed.

We went and got more pizza.

Every year, the Tuesday before Thanksgiving my aunt Ellen had a psychic medium come to her house to give individual readings. Ellen was raised Catholic but believed in past lives. She told me we traveled through each incarnation with the same people. In your next life your mother may return as your best friend. Your sister may be your husband. When you connect with someone instantly it's because you've known them before.

I finished my run and did crunches on the shag carpet. Music blasting, I hardly noticed Matt in the living room. His tooth-brush jutted from his mouth. He had slept in a teal T-shirt and black tapered sweatpants. The sweatpants ringed his ankles, accentuating his long pale feet. The way he walked around while brushing his teeth reminded me of a hummingbird dipping its beak into the same empty flower over and over and over.

He finished brushing and stood over me.

"I can't believe you already worked out!"

I wanted to tell him how running was the only thing that quieted my mind.

"It's good running weather," I said.

He sat down next to me.

"Do you always get up this early?"

Yes, because my mind races.

"I like to exercise before work sometimes."

"I wish I had that dedication."

I feel like I have no choice.

"It's not too hard. You just have to pack your gym bag the

73

night before." I started to stretch my legs. "God, I can't even touch my toes."

"Neither can I!"

He lunged his arms out and yelped at the strain, then rolled onto his side, arm bent, facing me. The pose revealed a portion of his pale, flat stomach.

We were quiet for a beat, a comfortable silence.

"You're in such good shape," he said, smiling. "I could never date someone in better shape than me."

But you. You're incredibly fit. Do you not see that?

I forced a laugh. "Why's that?"

"I'd feel constantly insecure. I'd, like, never want to eat again."

"Did you see that place we drove by last night? John's Drive-In? We need to get ice cream there."

"Great. You get two scoops. I'll have a side of air. Unless they have peanut butter cup. Then I'm getting a waffle cone."

I rolled over onto my side, too, my body sinking into the carpet's soft ropey tufts. "I could go for a Bloody Mary right now, to be honest."

"I could go for tequila."

"I could go for meth."

He laughed a deep, chocolaty laugh. A laugh that solidified our alliance. Then his voice dropped to just above a whisper.

"What do you want to do today?"

We made our plans.

The clouds and cold persisted. Everyone bundled up in hooded sweatshirts and left their bathing suits and tank tops in piles on their travel bags. The plan was to go to the Sloppy Tuna. It sounded like fun.

On rainy summer days in Springfield my cousins and I used to play Ninja Turtles. An old jump rope became nunchucks and a wood beam served as a bo staff. My cousin John Andrew was the oldest, the natural leader, so he was Leonardo. Mikey was good at building things, so he played Donatello, the Turtles' in-house engineer. Jay was always Raphael because he was the youngest, and I was Michelangelo, the party animal. My cousin Tommy, who was learning to walk, had to settle for Master Splinter or April O'Neil.

We'd play Ninja Turtles, then we'd watch the older cousins play Nintendo. *Super Mario Bros. 3* was a spectator sport, and I never dared ask for a controller. As Pat and John Andrew willed the mustachioed plumbers through Desert Land, smashing coin-filled blocks and snatching raccoon suits, Jay Bird and I would munch on Goldfish. Something about the familiarity of the game—the jumping, the stomping, the flying, the dying over and over—held me in its thrall. I cheered on my older cousins, idolizing their prowess as if they were professional athletes. It didn't matter that I didn't get to play. All that mattered was that we were there together, urging each other on toward the same eight-bit castle.

After my morning run, the Hive grew kinetic. The hiss of showers, the drumbeat of feet as housemates rushed up and down the stairs. A roar of hair dryers, and then a silence when they short-circuited the electricity, forcing Colby to the basement to jigger the fuse box.

"Don't worry, your dad's got it under control!" he called as he raced down the stairs.

I slipped on my leather boat shoes and followed Matt to the driveway. Cars were another invisible partition of the Hive, a signifier of cliques and alliances, of control. Shane, Colby, and Perrie were driving, and their cars filled quickly. Matt hopped in the back seat of Shane's Rover, four in the back already. I felt an elemental flush of panic, the kickball teams filling up. Matt nudged Taylor onto his lap.

"Come on," he called to me. "Plenty of room."

The Sloppy Tuna was a beachside bar clapped with gold shingles and fenced in by a wall of multicolored surfboards. In the patio I could see a few high-top tables and a small corner stage.

We were right by the beach, and the wind was stronger. It plastered my hair in mists of salt. I'd been in Montauk for thirty-six hours and had yet to see the breaking waves. I could see them now, and hear them. Compared to the waves from my childhood they felt larger, more violent, their crowns of spray at once majestic and feral.

At Mike's behest we posed for a group photo. I still have it. In it we're on the beach, arranged in an arm-wrapped row. Four people are crouched down, knees bent like a soccer team. We're posed in front of a white lifeguard chair affixed with an American flag pulled taut by the wind. A green tide flag flying below it means it's safe to swim, but the water's too cold and choppy. All of us are bundled in sweaters and light jackets, our cheeks still winter pale. We look happy and hopeful. We look relaxed. None of us knows what the summer will hold.

"You two come with me." Ashley dragged Matt and me to the inside bar, adorned with hanging light bulbs and a corrugated metal ceiling. The Sloppy Tuna was packed with a random assortment of Murray Hill bros and surfers in hooded ponchos. I felt an odd sense of recognition, one that would only heighten as the weekends layered. These people, though I'd never met them, looked somehow familiar. To Ashley they truly were.

"Hey, Ash!"

"Hey, girl!"

"What's up, Ashley?"

At the counter a group of guys—they looked like a bachelor party—were woofing through a round of Jameson. A sign above them read WHEN IT RAINS WE POUR.

If it was a beach day in Montauk, you got shitfaced. If it wasn't a beach day in Montauk, you got shitfaced. Ashley handed us Transfusions—Welch's grape juice, ginger ale, and vodka. I took a sip, the vodka warming my chest. It was delicious.

"Two rum punches!" Kirsten called, pointing to a drink in a yellow beach pail. She and Colby had been boozing at the house all morning. Kirsten was slurry and delightful, but Colby had grown taciturn. He kept checking Instagram and staring into nothing. Even in the few days of knowing him, I could tell by the way he swung from masculine to feminine, boisterous to insular, that he pendulumed toward extremes.

"We need to go upstairs before it gets to capacity," said Kirsten. "I don't want to wait in the line."

I followed Kirsten and Colby upstairs, where a large balcony overlooked the beach.

"Have fun last night?" I asked Kirsten.

"Ugh, I'm in a dark place," she said. "I hooked up with

Stefano again." She looked down at her phone. "And I told him to meet us here, but he hasn't responded."

"What's his deal?"

"I don't know. He grew up in Croatia, went to Harvard. He's very well-read. We talk about books a lot. He's just...intense."

"Intense how?"

"Like...he looks into my eyes. And I feel like he's penetrating my soul."

I nodded. But I had no idea what that was like. I asked her.

"It's uncomfortable. And exciting." The ocean wind was whipping her hair and she covered herself with her sweatshirt hood. "I don't know. Let's go inside and take a picture together. I want to geotag it so he knows where I am. I want him to see I'm having fun."

Ashley was standing against the balcony, getting quizzed on finance by D.Lo and Tyler. D.Lo worked as an interest rate analyst, and she was a rising star on her team. Tyler worked in foreign exchange, and his hours were grueling.

"Wait, so explain this to me: If a central bank is using foreign exchange currencies to stabilize the market, is the direct ask price reciprocal to the ask price or the bid price?"

"The ask price. But we normally do a cross rate against another..."

Ashley stopped listening. Someone had grabbed her attention across the bar. He was built like a swimmer: tall, broad, V-shaped with a face that looked wave-smoothened. He wore a red-and-blue Berkeley College windbreaker, khaki shorts, and Reef sandals. His hair—brown, thick, and wavy—looked like it could be at home in a hockey helmet.

She removed her sunglasses. They were big and round. The

shiny black frames caught her reflection as she clamped them shut in her hand. She nervously covered her mouth with her fist. "Ash?"

She was willing him over. Channeling his gaze through the crowds that were watching tennis on the outdoor TV. She was praying for him to approach. To ask her out. To take her to a wine bar in the West Village and share a chaste kiss on West Fourth Street, to let her slip away in a cab before he could do more. She'd leave him guessing and he'd text her back, ask her out again. In that moment he became the locus of her entire future.

As their eyes met she tried to convey that he had been cast in this role, that she didn't know him yet, but that she had the capacity to love him entirely.

"Do you see someone you recognize?" I asked.

"No. It was no one. Just some kid who looked like my brother."

I was introduced to a flurry of people. There were other houses, other names. Here was Sam from the Slide House. He grew up in Alabama. This was Madison. She stayed with Kirsten's friends in a place called the Mansion. Rivers's House (who was Rivers?) was currently sleeping thirty. The Tree House sat on the edge of Amagansett. The kids from Scrim House got evicted last summer. Don't ask.

At one point Colby finally looked up from his phone. A Villanova couple, Casey and Brendan, had corralled him. They wore baseball caps and matching shirts from Barry's Bootcamp. Colby introduced them to me, and I was disarmed by their alacrity. They were delving into the kind of chatty details usually reserved for very close friends.

"So how do you think the house is going to compare to your last summer?" asked Brendan "I remember you loved it."

I was about to correct him, but didn't. He had no idea I was new. He had folded me into his memories. He had assumed I was always a part of the Hive.

———————

Afternoon bled into night. A windy blur. Back at the house people napped on sinking air mattresses. The girls sardined three deep in the cold king-size bed. For dinner Shane cooked hot dogs on the grill. Smoke billowed up and mixed with the trees.

The Hive, with its strange rooms and curios, was beginning to remind me of my grandparents' apartment on Sorrento Street. Both homes spoke of incremental accrual. Preservation. Spin dial radios and paper plate holders of thatched bamboo. The Hive held a history that didn't yet belong to me, but I could feel myself adding to it, in the same way I had as a boy back in Springfield.

Pop-Pop had lived in the two-family house on Sorrento Street for eighty years of his life. His mother died in the 1918 flu epidemic, his father in a car accident. Orphaned at six months, he was raised by his three spinster aunts—Anna, Helen, and Murr. Anna was the secretary for the chief of police. Helen worked for a car dealership. Murr, who died before my mom was born, was the homemaker. I knew them only through their personal effects—a hand-stitched quilt, pendant lamps, old hat boxes— that continued to gild Sorrento Street into my childhood. Kicki preserved their heirlooms, and her own, with great care.

Kicki was a pack rat, but she never minded when we played with Sorrento Street's treasures. On Sundays we'd sift through her old things: porcelain birds, loose keys, a bronze baby shoe, costume jewelry, and a wooden dollhouse.

The top apartment was two stories, and the third floor, with its floral wallpaper and emerald-green runners, was a cache for ancient belongings. One day, bent on exploring, I ventured up there alone. I dipped into my old bedroom (we had lived on Sorrento Street until I was five) and entered the closet, running my hands through Helen's old mink coat. The space was sloped and shallow. If I stretched my arms I could almost reach across it. I pulled the light string, and something caught my eye.

Affixed to the back wall was a tiny metal slide bolt, and above it, a cabin hook. I squatted down, discovering a small square door. I couldn't believe I'd never noticed it before, but the sight of it sent my heart thrumming. I unclasped the bolt and the door slowly opened. I found myself staring into a small dark room.

For a six-year-old, there could be no greater discovery. A secret crawl space. A door just my size. I ran to Kicki to show her. She knew of the crawl space, of course, but played into my excitement. It was too dangerous to enter—the floor beams were rickety and spiked with nails. But Kicki devised the perfect solution.

"Let's peer in with a flashlight," she suggested.

Together we illuminated the dark.

My mom, too, had known of the hidden door. When she was a girl she'd shared a bedroom with her sister Bambi. On summer nights they could hear the roar of a lion that lived in the Forest Park Zoo. The zoo sat within walking distance, and they loved to visit the animals. Peacocks, buffalo, Morganetta the elephant, a polar bear named Snowball, and Jiggs the monkey, who would spit on his onlookers. But when the lion's roar carried through the dark, they'd lie awake, pinned to their beds, picturing the lion breaking out of his cage, clawing through the park, finding his way to Sorrento Street.

On those hot summer nights only one thought brought them comfort. If the lion ever escaped, they knew exactly where they'd hide.

The door became a scrim for my games of make-believe, but it also hinted toward a more capacious reality. Even a dwelling as fixed as Sorrento Street could be filled with secret rooms. Before my grandparents moved, I took a picture of the hidden door. I wanted to remember it was there.

———————

The pregame for Sunday was themed *The Great Gatsby*. The movie remake had just come out and we blasted the Fergie song from the soundtrack, "A Little Party Never Killed Nobody." The girls wore black flapper dresses and scarves in their hair. The guys did linen shirts and pocket squares. We pretended we were in East Egg and drank with abandon.

Later, we went back to town. Across the street from the Mem stood a bar called the Point. It was a bit brighter and I liked it better. Warm wood walls trapped the heat and the sound. You had no choice but to dance. We formed a circle in the heart of the bar. The girls leaned into the two big floor fans, pretending to be Beyoncé.

When we were done at the Point they stamped our arms so we could come back. We crossed the street to the Mem, kicked back shots, and danced to the live band. We went back to the Point, then back to the Mem again, shuttling between the bars like a beachside game of running bases.

I stayed out late, until the sky glowed purple. I danced with a few girls, but none who showed interest. At bars, at clubs, I mostly struck out. I had experienced a single one-night stand since moving to New York. A girl with a crop of pyramids tattooed on her neck.

Matt had left around two a.m., stopping first for pizza. I found myself wishing I had left with him.

When I got home the kitchen lights were on, but everyone was asleep. The remnants of our Gatsby party looked sad and garish—cigarette butts, whiskey bottles, smashed lime rinds, and wine globes stained red. A disaster of chips and pretzel sticks sanded the Formica. I was too tired to start cleaning. The kitchen was equipped with an unusual number of light switches, and I flicked through each one.

I went down to the basement and was about to open the door to the Game Room, but stopped. I heard rustlings and moans. I creaked the door open just a bit and light spilled across the futon. An unzipped sleeping bag was bobbing up and down.

I was about to shut the door when Colby's head popped out. His gelled hair had come unlocked. He squinted, face flushed, eyes red.

"Oh son, I'm sorry, is this your bed?"

The kid beneath him, I recognized, was Brendan from the

Sloppy Tuna, the one who had confused me for a second-summer Hiver. I'd thought he was dating the girl he was with. Hell, I realized, maybe he still was. I gave a quick wave and shut the door.

"I can't believe I'm saying this, but I'm ready to get the hell back to the city." Matt was standing in the living room with his duffel, waiting for Timmy to finish packing. I felt the same. Three days of drinking had left me anxious and rattled. I needed to leave Montauk as quickly as possible.

Timmy thundered up the stairs. "Matt, ya ready, let's get the fuck out of here, bye everyone, have a great week."

Timmy blared out the door and Matt turned to me. "Well, looks like I'm off."

"When are you out again?"

"In a few weeks."

"Cool. I'll be out here."

"Great. Well, I'll see you." He leaned in for a hug, two arms, an embrace more solid than a three-day friendship might otherwise merit. But it still felt oddly insufficient. I attributed our instant connection to the boisterous atmosphere of the Hive, friendships coalescing in a vortex. When he left, I felt an absence. I was glad we had become good friends.

That night, back in Tribeca, I got in bed but couldn't sleep. I cracked open Rachel Kushner's *The Flamethrowers* but got tripped up by the language. I turned off the lights and the ceiling glowed blue.

The joy of the weekend dissolved, and dark peregrinations of thought took hold. I was compulsively afraid of dying alone, and now that fear began to animate a waking nightmare. I pictured myself as an old man, living in a basement apartment in an isolated neighborhood, my parents, the only people who loved me unconditionally, long dead. I had passed through life without finding true love. An existence devoid of physical passion and intimacy. I failed in my career, I never had children, I no longer had any hint of a family. Life had moved quickly, beyond my grasp, and it would only continue to get worse until I died and there was nothing.

These dark visions lacked an origin. They simply were, and while I lived with these impressions every moment of my life, they usurped my thoughts when I was at my most vulnerable. The effects of drinking had reduced my defenses, and the bad thoughts were unrelenting. I couldn't stop them. I could only hope to replace them. That night, for the first time, I replaced them with thoughts of Matt.

Chapter Ten

The next weekend was our five-year college reunion. I took Friday off and drove up to Boston with Mike.

"Waze says take the Merritt, but Google says to take Ninety-Five."

"What's Apple say?" I asked.

"Apple thinks we're in Ohio."

"Go with Waze."

We drove beneath the Merritt's ornate stone overpasses and chatted about the Hive. I told Mike I loved it, that I was sad not to be there. I also told him I'd been nervous. I'd never been in a group of so many gay people. I didn't know where I'd fall. He told me not to worry, that I fit in well.

"Colby told me last week that you're his new favorite housemate. He thinks you're hilarious. Plus you have a six-pack. When did you get that, by the way?"

The Hive had been exhilarating, but I also wondered if my sleepless Monday night was a common Montauk side effect. Did everyone return to the city in a halo of dread? I kept this thought to myself.

"I have two abs at most," I said. "Look, there's a McDonald's. Pull over and I'll make them disappear completely."

Mike and I had met the first week of freshman year. He was like me, a planner, a corraller. I'd walk down the hall to pregame in his large corner room. He made every new visitor sign his wall with a Sharpie. By the end of the year he had collected hundreds of names.

His room had a huge black sandal tacked to the wall. It was a Mike's Hard Lemonade promo, the kind of thing you'd see in a liquor store. His friends from home had stolen it for him. His goal freshman year was to assemble a cohort as solid as them. He became the architect of our friend group, just as he was the architect of the Hive. Sculpting. Discerning. Quietly pulling people in and cutting others out.

When Mike came out to me, I was happy for him. He had never been attracted to girls, he admitted. He always knew he was somehow different. Mike and I had spent all of college bemoaning our singlehood. He'd figured out his bulwark and removed it. That year he was buoyed with optimism, with possibility. I remember envying him for that. Hoping that someday it would be my turn.

We lived in a six-man "mod" that year, a beer-drenched townhouse. We called Mike's room the revolving door. Every night was a Kelly Clarkson concert. He was embracing his sexuality. I knew that something wasn't working for me, but I also knew that I was not wired like Mike. I enjoyed having sex with girls. I just needed to meet the right one.

We drove through lower campus, passing the gothic stone dorms, the church, the Plex, the dining hall. Our football stadium was bannered in gold. It stood so high it blocked the sun. The few remaining summer students looked impossibly young, their knees bony, their expressions unburdened, their backpacks full.

We checked into Edmonds Hall and received a white card with a room code. Sheets and pillows were folded neatly at the foot of each bed. A welcome agenda detailed breakfasts, barbecues, dances, and Mass. I was rooming with Mike, my Tribeca roommate Evan, and our friend Mallory. The dorm felt unchanged. White brick walls, sturdy furniture, a gray carpet soaked in decades' worth of beer. I made my bed just as I had years before, the white sheet unfurling and catching the sun.

The weekend was exhilarating but surreal. Time bent in odd ways. Five years dissolved, then stretched to a chasm. On Saturday I ate grilled chicken and pasta salad under a big stretched tent, the heat beating against my neck. I spoke with people I'd seen every day for four years, then not again. The exchanges followed a pattern. What are you up to, where are you living, who do you still see, are you dating, are you married, are you nowhere near ready to have kids, what are your plans for tonight, and then, as the conversation neared its natural end, the sad realization that, despite our shared history, despite the time we got written up together for funneling beers in our sweatpants, this was probably it for another five years, or ever.

At the end of the barbecue I ran into my college girlfriend Betsy. She was living in Texas and working for a tech company.

"Oh, and I have a boyfriend! We've been together for nearly a year."

I smiled, the announcement threading its way through my

own personal failures. As I walked back to the dorm I thought about why it was that, even though I'd gone deeper with Betsy emotionally than with anyone else, my feelings had still seemed insufficient.

It just takes the right girl, my dad always said.

Mike had assembled a thirty-five-minute video collage from our college years. He invited a couple dozen of us to the cabaret room in Vanderslice Hall and rigged his laptop to a projector. The cabaret room had high ceilings and big windows that reflected the sunset as the movie showed. The video began with freshman year, a slapdash of photos and video clips from Mike's vast archive. It moved chronologically. An unfolding of our four years, the best times, the funny drunk moments we forgot. Underage sake bombing. Case races. Endless pregames and drunk dancing to the "Call on Me" music video. A random Monday night, heart of winter, when we went out and pushed each other into snow banks. In one video clip I'm passed out with my head in a toilet. Mike flushes it to wake me up.

In so many of the clips and photos, we're hugging or embracing each other. We're constantly laughing. The rooms are full, never less than seven or eight of us clutching Busch Lights with two hands. The video is set to music: "Such Great Heights." "Mr. Brightside." "Man in Motion." The soundtrack of our college years. We have longer hair, we're pink from spring break, we're never alone. We are all so young, but of course we don't realize this. We're all so good to each other. We know that we're going to travel through life together. For the most part we do.

That night, we threw an after-party in our four-man suite. I connected my click-wheel iPod to a set of Bose speakers and played a song I'd heard the weekend before in Montauk. It was a Chvrches remix of an MS MR song called "Hurricane." The original is morose, but the remix is fizzy, contorting the pain into euphoric release.

Soon our cloistered room filled with people, everyone caffeinated by the backdrop. I controlled the music, read the crowd. We had reverted back to college—shotgunning beers, tossing empties against the wall. Random couples making out in the kitchen. I kept playing the music.

My head throbbed and the room began to shrink. People were literally lining up to get in. It reminded me of our epic college parties, the way, with a few spidered texts, we could commandeer a night. I kept watching the crowd erupt with each new song as though they were attached by a network of strings.

I pressed play on Icona Pop's "I Love It," went into my bedroom, and shut the door. Out the window a light illuminated the townhouse I'd lived in senior year. The lyrics *I don't care / I love it* thrashed through the door over and over.

I sat on my bed and drank a Bud Light. I felt locked in place, physically unable to move. A sea of people, a cotillion of Solo cups. I was back where I started.

Mike came in, one eye lidded, pink Lacoste shirt dashed with beer. I watched the delayed reaction, the way his squinched face rolled from confusion to assessment to pulses of concern. He sat down next to me.

"What's up, bud?"

I didn't know. I didn't fucking know. I lived a blessed life. I was currently surrounded by my closest friends. All of it just made me feel worse.

I started to speak, but couldn't. A cheer erupted from the common room, the result of a flip cup game. I leaned my head on Mike's shoulder. In college he was my rock. We'd fight like brothers—shouts, curses—then midscuffle we'd burst out laughing.

In a sea of people, I'd never felt more alone. I told him so.

He said he knew the feeling.

———

The table was capillaried with empty beers—Natty Light, Busch, Bud—crunched paper racks, Solo cups, a half-drunk bottle of Jameson. Cold lo mein congealed in a styrofoam shell.

I had somehow passed out in my clothes. Mike and Mallory were still asleep, but Evan had left early to go to his girlfriend's law school graduation.

In the corner of the room, pressed against the wall, lay a maroon can of Tab. We had no idea where it came from or how someone had even acquired it.

I walked into the bathroom. It was hewn with the kind of thin beige walls you could accidentally punch a hole through. Empty beer cans rimmed the sink. Toothpaste had dried and crusted over the drain. Across the mirror someone had written I DON'T CARE in puffs of blue shaving cream. I took a photo of it. Then I went about picking up the empties.

Chapter Eleven

Penn Station on a summer Friday was exciting and strangulating. The ceilings seemed to compress, the lights to shriek. Windowless vestibules had the time-bending capacity of a casino.

In the catacomb-like halls I wove past affluent travelers armed with Filson bags and golf clubs and pugs in soft carriers. The heat affixed everything with a layer of agitation. I raced through the station, passing bodegas, beer buckets, the Starbucks with its rivers of AC. I loosened my collar. I rolled up my sleeves. Sweat lashed my shirt beneath my bag's thick arm straps. At Penn Station I was always running late, always racing the clock. I hit play on my Montauk playlist and scrambled to my platform.

The train to Montauk transferred at Jamaica. I gazed out the window at the Queens cityscape, the blur of brick apartments, the replicating latticework of rusted fire escapes. Train tracks stretched across an elevated platform eye level with trees and rooftops. The streets filled with traffic below. On one passing rooftop sat a lone plastic chair. I imagined what it was like to sit there on a hot day, watching the trains pass one by one.

I watched Archer Avenue stream by below: a Liberty Tax, a Chicken and Pizza, a shuttered unisex barber shop. The yellow awning of a China King Express was faded and stained like a truck tire's mud flap. The train slowed, absorbing the view. Then, just before the details came into focus, before anyone could figure out just where they were, Queens disappeared behind the platform, the station's flat metal awning blocking the light.

People stood, eyes alert, bags tucked beneath their arms. The transfer train sat ready across the platform. In a moment, the walkway would become a gauntlet, a press of bodies, everyone jockeying. Those who moved too slow were doomed to stand on the next train for an hour or more.

Two tight-faced women were shoving their way through the aisle. Their bone-thin arms were draped with purses, nothing else. Light travel, I'd learn, was a kind of status symbol. A nod to permanent wardrobes and second homes. The women pushed to the front of the door, complaining loudly. For some, the indignity of public transit was just too much to bear.

The doors hissed open, and a stampede struck the platform. I rode through the crowds as if in a murmuration, swinging and swooping, dropping low to catch a view of the new train through its windows. Many passengers were already nested, unwrapping their chicken Caesar wraps and tapping their Kindles. I boarded amid a sea of people. Movement slowed. Couples pointed across the aisles, scouting for open seats together. By the time I got to the aisle, the seats and staircases were full. I fashioned my bag into a chair and opened *And the Mountains Echoed* by Khaled Hosseini. Montauk was three hours away.

When I got to the Hive that evening, Mike, Ashley, and Kirsten were already there. The porch off the master bedroom overlooked the driveway, and they called to me. Ashley and Mike were smoking cigarettes in their workout gear. Kirsten held a stem of wine.

The three of them had the deepest history. A shared childhood in Fairfield. A world before our own.

<LI_SB>My own friendships from home were bedrock. I'd met my two best friends, Ryan and Bryan, on the first day of kindergarten, and my other best friend, Dave, on the first day of middle school. Every morning we biked to school together, a bounding pack of neon helmets, the autumn air rushing past the sides of our cheeks.

As we grew older we discovered alcohol. First Smirnoff Ice, then cheap vodka and Keystone Light. Our crew expanded to include girls: Jodi and Jocelyn and Kara and Annie. We drank in the woods or on the backs of people's cars or on a small uninhabited island in the middle of the Connecticut River. We always assigned a designated driver, we always looked out for one another. Even as our paths diverged geographically and socially, we were still best friends.

———

That night, we pregamed in the living room to a mix on my iPod. Twenty-three of us total, buzzed and scrubbed clean. A deck of cards fanned on the coffee table. Ashley and Kirsten. Mike, Colby, Timmy. D.Lo and Perrie. The finance bros. We were coalescing, escaping things together. I sensed my veins warm, my shoulders slacken. The city felt far away.

On a wicker table lay Matt's green sweatshirt. He must've forgotten it over Memorial Day.

"Where's Matt this weekend?" I asked Mike.

"Not sure, he might've stayed in Manhattan. Or maybe he went to Fire Island? I can't remember."

Whenever I thought about Matt I felt an unfamiliar tug in my chest. It was strange, but if he couldn't be in Montauk, I wanted him to be in Manhattan that weekend. I wanted him to be alone or with a few girlfriends watching *The First Wives Club* on TBS because he had a christening the next day in Brooklyn he couldn't get out of. I didn't want to picture him on Fire Island.

"He's great, isn't he?" Mike said.

"Totally. I miss having him here."

"Ha, I know, right? Me too."

It rankled, I didn't know why. Something about Mike's response, the way he'd laughed a bit, smiled, then took a sip of his vodka soda. I didn't know what I expected. I didn't know what I wanted him to say. But I knew that the way I had begun to miss Matt was different. It pulled like an undertow. It felt like a small hole had been drilled into me.

I woke early the next morning; I couldn't sleep. I was assigned to the big bedroom in the basement, Bedroom 4. It was windowless, like a closed-off cabin. I'd been too drunk to turn off the bedside lamp, and it bathed the pinewood walls in a warm, honeyed glow.

I spotted Shane in the driveway through the dirt-splattered window in the hall. He was already dressed and showered, his hair parted, his shirt tucked in. He was washing his Land Rover with a thick yellow bone sponge. I watched as the soap trickled through the brush guard and frothed at his feet. When he was done, he streak-dried the windshield with a squeegee.

I walked outside to join him. We were the only ones up, we both needed coffee.

"Let's go to the Montauk Bake Shoppe," he said. "Hop in."

Shane worked on a trading floor in fixed income sales. His office was situated in the heart of Times Square. At night, when darkness fell, the blinking signs of M&M'S World bathed his desk in cloying light. He wore an Oxford suit, a Brooks Brothers non-iron shirt, an Hermès tie. His shoes were polished. His hair was combed. His desk space held three computer screens. He had worked there for three years and was completely in the closet to almost all of his coworkers.

Shane woke each morning at 5:45 flooded with dark thoughts. The mornings were the worst. How could he keep doing this? How could he keep pretending? Not just that he was straight, but that he actually liked his job. That he could do this indefinitely.

To work was to suffer. He knew this, he accepted it. But there had to be more.

One of Shane's gay friends, a buddy from Montauk, sat a few desks away. Sometimes the gay friend would come over, say hi, his voice carrying. Shane's shoulders would scrunch, his spine would bolt, his words chilling to ice.

Shane and I were not natural friends. He cared about things I did not. He knew how things were built and built well. A penchant for quality ran in his blood. His grandfather once managed the finest silver company in New England.

He sought power in stasis, in custom, tradition. At the Ditch Plains parking lot he'd point out the Land Rover Defenders, informing whoever was around that the vehicles accrued in value each year. He had a calm, neutral voice. He walked through the house with a masculine broadness, a strong neck. His green eyes were rimmed with soft sunken circles. His small nose and sharp chin lent him a regal maturity. He took Propecia and his blond hair stopped receding.

Shane, like me, was an only child. Space and silence, for us, were Janus-headed. He was always watering the plants, arranging the deck furniture, finding new spaces for the beach chairs and Kadima sets. I recognized the instinct, the quick bursting need for a solitary pursuit, a stepping away from the mayhem of inclusion. And its opposite: how a dinner alone, in front of the TV, could instill a dread so potent it cinched the lungs.

Shane was more closed off than I was, more discerning, more tart with new people. In middle school he got called a faggot and was barricaded in the locker room. He knew that his bully did not come from money, so he made a point to accumulate the best of everything, to show him he was better.

Shane was handsome and doting. He was immensely loyal. We'd chafe at each other like brothers, nip at the other's heels. But as only children we understood each other on a molecular level.

He drove us along the Old Montauk Highway, past the Beachcomber and the windmill and the three yellow smiley faces painted on the side of the Oceanside Beach Resort. In the car we rehashed the night. At the Mem, Colby had gotten blackout drunk. He had made out with a dude in the middle of the dance floor. The dude had gone to school with Ashley. Worlds were constantly colliding.

The gay scene in Montauk was not like the gay scene in Fire Island, Shane explained. There were lots of gays in Montauk for sure, but no designated gay events or spaces.

"The Mem is a gay bar. The Point is a gay bar. Every bar in Montauk can be a gay bar. Just ask Colby."

To Shane—so convincingly straight at work, yet so openly gay in his private life—the signposts of heterosexuality were nothing but. Even the straightest guy in Montauk could be just like him.

The Montauk Bake Shoppe (known to locals as the Bakery) was wedged between a liquor store and a surf shop in a row of old storefronts. Down the street sat a boutique owned by an actress from the television show *Hey Dude*. A sign in the Bake Shoppe window read TRY OUR FAMOUS JELLY CROISSANTS. It was written in black Sharpie and tacked next an old mimeographed printout that read BEST COFFEE IN TOWN. Inside, the glass counter contained doughnuts, cheese danishes, muffins, and cookies shaped like lobsters.

I ordered an egg sandwich and an iced coffee, which came with a plastic domed lid. Shane got a slice of quiche. The girl behind the counter spoke in a thick Irish brogue. Most of the workers were young, younger than Shane and me, and European. Our clerk shouted "Egg up!" toward the kitchen. She gave Shane the last of the jelly croissants.

The Hive, Shane explained, was not an accurate reflection of the gay world in Manhattan. Most of the gay guys Shane encountered were superficial and stuck-up. They hid their insecurities beneath designer clothing. They judged everyone around them. They talked shit. They lied. They betrayed. They fucked the whole town.

At one party, a group of guys had rented Range Rovers to drive from Chelsea to an apartment on the Upper West Side. It didn't matter that they all lived a short cab ride away. It was about the appearance.

I silently took this in. I wanted to point out that Shane himself was driving a Land Rover back to his Hamptons share house. But then again, he was giving me a ride in it.

The Hell's Kitchen gays were "tragic." The Brooklyn gays were "out there." The Chelsea gays were "queens." The West Village gays were "dicks." Gay guys who were actually good people, who were fun and adjusted and only slightly damaged, were as rare as unicorns.

He didn't look at me as he was saying this. He kept his eyes glued ahead. I wondered if he could read my thoughts, if he knew how I was struggling with my own Gordian knot of feelings. I wondered if he was trying to scare me.

"It's honestly terrible. There is nothing more depressing than being a single gay man in New York City."

"I can only imagine," I said.

Shane put on a song called "Second Summer" by Yacht. The lyrics were about a couple's second summer together. The singer questions whether the physics of their love can endure. The song is up-tempo but haunting, the vocals esoteric, the lyrics artless enough for the listener to graft meaning.

"So where are they?" I asked as the song ended, half in jest. "Where are the unicorns? The elusive good gays?"

The windows were down and the breeze whipped Shane's hair. His sunglasses reflected the scroll of the sea.

"The Hive," he said without taking his eyes off the road.

That Saturday was our first true beach day. When Shane announced it was time to go, the house shook to life. The girls donned bikinis and cover-ups. The guys wore Vilebrequin bathing suits and board shorts from Saturdays surf shop.

I remembered waking early on the day of our family's beach vacation and packing my things in an old canvas bag. I was sentimental from a young age, imbuing my belongings with emotional value. I packed my favorite blankie, second-favorite blankie, and third-favorite blankie. My Cabbage Patch dolls Bronson and Emily and my teddy bear Poppy. I spent the week dragging them around our small rental cottage. These treasures were my entrée into worlds of make-believe, and my first and strongest bulwark against the creeping hands of loneliness. I couldn't bear the thought of them being alone and feeling the same way.

I drove into town with Perrie, my coworker. Since Memorial Day our boundaries had dissolved, and we'd frequently meet in her office to talk about our personal lives. Our roles at Scribner were divergent enough to prevent awkwardness. In the first weekend at the Hive I'd learned Perrie was a history buff. On our drive to the beach that day she gave me an overview of Montauk.

"See that? That's the Second House Museum. It's the oldest standing house in Montauk, from the seventeen hundreds. The railroad didn't even come out here until almost two hundred years later. It was just a fishing village until Carl Fisher came."

She pointed to the Tudor revival buildings on Main Street that were designed by the aforementioned Fisher, an American entrepreneur. He had planned to turn Montauk into a Miami Beach of the north, constructing a manor, a surf club, a yacht club, and polo and golf clubs all in the same Tudor style.

"Then the Depression hit. He never completed it. But that's why you see some of these stylized Tudor buildings. Including that huge apartment complex on the plaza."

I liked the idea that Montauk was not fully finished. Its architectural DNA was in a constant state of becoming, the old and the new existing in harmony.

"What about the Hive?" I joked. "Something tells me that was not a Carl Fisher original."

"Let's be honest," Perrie said, her window down, her red hair floating about, "the person who built the Hive was Mike."

The beach by the Sloppy Tuna was burbling with life that day. Knots of people lay beneath wind-popped umbrellas. Everyone looked young and fit, eyes scoping, ready.

We carried our beach chairs, passing by games of Spikeball and Kadima. Frisbees clattered into buckets for KanJam, the echoes of songs carrying from one Bose speaker to the next. I followed the others, who seemed to have a set destination. We kept close to the dunes, passing the lifeguard tower and the two volleyball courts where a lone girl roughed it up with a group of sand-caked guys.

"There's Volleyball Girl," Mike said. "She's always there."

We arranged the chairs in a semicircle, laying our towels in the middle. A communal tote held magazines, sports equipment, and a variety of sunscreens. We doused each other's backs, we shivered from the cream's coldness. This was the Hive's spot, I learned, beyond the volleyball nets. Some days, when the tide was strong, the waves formed a shelf of sand, and we'd sit right on the edge, sliding heels-first into the surf when the sun got too hot.

People came and went throughout the day. A revolving door of college friends, city friends, friends from other houses. Visitors fresh from the ocean dried off on our blankets. Housemates journeyed into town for iced coffee, for bags of chips. Others came back with cold cuts from Herb's Market, turkey stacked so high you had to angle your jaw to eat it.

"Be careful," warned Kirsten. "The seagulls here are bold as fuck. Last year I was eating a tuna sandwich and one came and stole it out of my hand."

She handed me a two-liter soda bottle filled with a pink mixed drink.

"What's this?" I asked.

"Tina Juice. It's better just to drink it and not ask questions."

Each of us took a swig.

Ashley sat on the towel next to me, a football by her side. She was reapplying tanning oil across her chest.

"You know how I paid for these?" she asked me, staring down at her cleavage. "Tennis lessons."

I laughed.

"Honest to God. Thirty bucks an hour. Took me two summers."

She caught sight of something over my shoulder and leaned over to Perrie, whispering in her ear. They both walked to the tide line.

Ashley couldn't stop thinking about the guy from the Sloppy Tuna, the one she'd locked eyes with over Memorial Day weekend, the one who'd smiled from across the deck but never approached. She'd been on the lookout for him ever since.

Sloppy Tuna Guy didn't appear that day, but within seconds a tall, ab-shredded man approached her. He was broad-shouldered and handsome, with dark hair wet from the ocean.

"Oh my God, it's you!" he said. "I feel like I see you everywhere! At Ruschmeyer's, at Surf Lodge."

They spoke for a few minutes. Then they started tossing the football.

Perrie returned to her towel.

"This is her thing," she said, adjusting her yellow frilled bikini. "She sees a guy, she stands by the water, they toss the football. If he has a good spiral, he's in. If not, she's not interested."

We watched as the guy caught Ashley's pass. He set the laces and released. The ball wobbled and quivered in a loose arc.

Perrie and I swapped dubious glances. "Not a prayer," I said.

Sloppy Tuna Beach was nothing like the beaches of my childhood. The crowd was rowdier, the surf more daunting. As a kid I spent the last week in June on the other side of the Sound, at Hawk's Nest Beach in Old Lyme, Connecticut. Twenty of us nestled into two cottages raised on stilts. My mother had gone to Hawk's Nest as a girl. My grandmother, too.

The beach there crackled with slipper shells and big flaps of seaweed. A barnacled jetty daggered the sea, corralling tides. The waves on the Long Island Sound were less waves than the scalloped suggestions of waves—the perfect tideline for a bluster of small cousins. At low tide the beach revealed its treasures— a shoreline backfilled with glimmers of sea glass, and fusillade from the beachside Pavilion bar in Sound View.

When the cousins and I built sandcastles, we'd patrol the sand for cigarette butts and use them as turrets.

Our cottages were porous and timeworn. Polynesian art and old rattan furniture decorated the living rooms, which opened to small screened-in porches. The attic bedrooms where my cousins and I slept had metal beds and low, sloping ceilings. We'd lie awake, listening to the sounds of our parents laughing and playing cards into the night.

As our family expanded, we needed more sleeping space. Rather than rent a third cottage, my aunt Ellen packed a tent, positioning it as a reward. If we cousins were good we could sleep in the tent. If we misbehaved we had to sleep inside. The tent was pitched in the front yard, and sound carried. In our canvas sleeping bags my cousins and I spoke in whispers, suppressing our laughter in the down of our pillows.

One night, too wired to sleep, we dared each other to venture to the beach, a hundred yards down the street. I was ten years old and felt bold. I accepted the dare. To prove I had made it, I had to bring back a handful of sand.

I unzipped the tent and felt my skin electrify. I was the good kid. I never got in trouble. I wasn't yet familiar with the thrill of rule-breaking, the adrenal rush that floods the senses. I walked by rows of dark cottages, their stilted underbellies like black yawning mouths. The street felt etched with danger, and I suddenly realized I was quite alone.

The beach stood at the foot of the street, and as I got close I could hear sounds. A fire came into view. There were all sorts of people on the sand.

I remember intuiting that the people by the fire were deviant. But something called me to them. I darted to one of the waterfront cottages and crawled beneath its stilts. I watched the scene, my belly pressed to the sand. Someone threw a beer bottle into the ocean. Music played from a boom box. I remember seeing two guys holding hands.

I lay there, still as a stone, hiding, observing. For a few minutes I had stepped outside the world of my cousins into something else, I didn't know what. I was watching from afar.

I returned to the tent, the sand falling from my open palm.

We drank through the afternoon and went to a day party at Cyril's fish shack until six. By the time I got home, my body craved sleep. I dozed off to the hum of towels spinning in the dryer.

I'm not sure how long I rested. Five minutes, a half hour. I was cocooned on the futon when my nostrils flared. The scent of burning flooded my sinuses, popped my eyes open, ringing every alarm in my brain. I flung off my blanket in a hot panic.

I started running up the stairs toward the smell of smoke. My mind was screaming. Someone must have fallen asleep smoking. Someone must've knocked over a candle. I reached the landing and could barely see. Sheets of smoke rolled across the living room.

The Hive was on fire.

The alarm began to sound, puncturing my ears.

I barreled into the living room. The smoke was chuffing out of the fireplace, webbing across the ceiling, sinking over the entire floor.

I stood inert. In my earliest childhood nightmare, I'm standing outside my house with my mom and Kicki, watching a fire bloom in my bedroom. I try to get my mom's attention, but she and Kicki are talking and won't listen. They don't see the fire. Only I do. Fire was my recurring fear.

Through the smoke I spotted Shane sprinting through the kitchen. He was carrying two plastic bottles. A loud hiss, more smoke, a subsiding heat as the fireplace went dark. The smoke began to disperse.

Shane swatted at the air above the fire alarm until it went off. He was still in his beach attire—a lacrosse pinny and neon green Chubbies.

"Whoops!" he said drunkenly. I realized he had put the fire out with seltzer water. From the SodaStream.

"Shane, why the hell were you building a fire!"

He was mopping up the ash with a beach blanket that read IT'S JITNEY, BITCH. He mentioned something about the house being cold, the flue not fully opening. I didn't care. I was just relieved the Hive hadn't burned down.

While I stood frozen, Shane had averted a crisis like we all would that summer—with a vodka mixer.

Chapter Twelve

Ashley started selecting her weekend outfits on Monday. She cataloged her tank tops and vintage cut-offs, she paired her bandage dresses with stilettos. By Tuesday she thought about being skinny for the beach. She ate kale salad and grilled chicken and fish, or she didn't eat. She cold-cleaned her skinny jeans in the freezer. At night when she craved ice cream, she went into the bathroom and inspected her body instead. She did SoulCycle every day, sometimes twice a day. She went to the hard instructors like Rique and Akin and Taye. Mike was working part-time at the Union Square location and would let her ride for free.

Ashley did financial research for a real estate developer based in Fairfield. She worked alone in an office suite on Madison Avenue. The office next to hers still had the faded impression of furniture—dust rings, carpet indents, a rectangle on the wall where a painting had hung. An abandoned golf putter and a handful of golf balls sprawled across the seafoam carpet in the hallway. She'd look at the putter each morning, wondering why it had been left behind.

She spent her lunch breaks searching for light. She knew the movement of the sun and the best spots to find it. From 11:00 to 11:35, the tables by the Central Park Apple Store. At noon it was Park Avenue down by Grand Central. At one p.m., the outdoor area across from the GM building. Casa Lever on Fifty-Third and Park, early afternoon but not past two. After two, the fountains on Fifty-Third or a small square outside of the Blackstone building.

We had all purchased half shares, eight weekends total. But Ashley went to the Hive every weekend, whether it was assigned to her or not. No one questioned this. No one wanted it any other way.

During that same week I hunkered down, worked late, read manuscripts in bed. I threw myself into work to keep my mind occupied. The dark thoughts had not dissipated. I could be washing my hands or waiting on the platform for the C train, and an anxious shame would gather in my chest, sometimes making it hard to breathe. I continued to construct a future in which I was alone and unloved. I felt a level of self-loathing that blinkered my vision. Before Montauk the possibility of love, to my mind, had all but dissolved.

But something had shifted. New building materials arrived. I was pulling down beams, letting in some light, crumpling up the blueprints that no longer made sense. I was still anxious, still painfully insecure. But a new trace of hope wove through those late June days, bringing me back to the freedom I felt during the first few days of summer as a kid. A breeze off the river, the shine of sunglasses, marble buildings cast in warm melon light. With the heat came a sense of opportunity, a return to the days when anything might be possible. That night in Tribeca my roommates came home to pack their overnight bags and meet up with their girlfriends, and our apartment was hot and still and quiet. I stepped out on the deck and packed a bowl, admiring the rectangles of light from the windows on Duane Street. I took a hit and sank into a chair, listening to the spectral chime of the ice cream truck below. I texted Matt.

Matt and I were becoming friends outside of the Hive. On Wednesdays I'd open my Gmail, awaiting the weekend room assignments. Sometimes his name would appear on my Gchat list, and I'd scroll across it to reveal his avatar. In it he wore a pink polo. His hair was longer and swept to the side. We'd chat for a few minutes, then I'd go invisible. A longer exchange, even through a screen's cold remove, made me flushed and anxious. Matt would appear and disappear, too, going idle for hours only to resurface with a few rapid-fire comments, then disappearing again. Doors opening and closing all day.

On Friday, my coworker Whitney taught me the shortcut to Montauk. The trick was like a warp pipe in *Super Mario*. If you caught the originating train from Hunter's Point in Queens, you could bypass Penn Station and the elbow-slash at Jamaica. You could leave work later and still get there with time for an iced coffee at the bodega. Best of all, you were guaranteed a seat.

I was staring out the window at the Hampton Bays water tower when Matt texted me. See you tonight :)

As the train pulled into Montauk station, I could feel the strictures unbinding. I was in a different world, a summer world, a world baked by the sun. I felt a breathless anticipation as I walked down the platform, a journey protracted by the slow clod of weekenders shouldering leather bags.

Mike had been out running errands and was waiting for me in the parking lot. Kirsten and Ashley were already at the house. D.Lo and Perrie were on their way.

"Shane's driving out with Colby," Mike said. "We got in a huge fight last night. We were out to dinner with Tyler and Timmy and he got blackout drunk and fell asleep on his plate."

Shane had always enjoyed getting after it, but lately his drinking had noticeably escalated.

"I feel like it's partially my fault," Mike continued. "He's miserable at work. He hates living in Stuytown. When I quit my job to start my company I promised I'd support him. Now the company's failing, I'm working at SoulCycle, and he's stuck picking up the extra rent."

Mike had quit his marketing job two years earlier to start his own social media search engine. The idea was to aggregate content and influencers and quantify the impact of tweets and Instagram and Facebook posts. Mike woke up each morning, made coffee in his Keurig, and followed up with beta users while watching Kathie Lee and Hoda. His developer had set up the back end so that he could go in and see what people were searching. He'd look for observable patterns and figure out how to build a smarter search.

When Klout came along, his product became redundant. His

start-up had failed, his investors were losing money, and his entrepreneurial dreams were dead. That summer Mike was desperately trying to sell the company.

He asked me when Matt was coming. I told him he was taking the Cannonball.

"I saw him last Thursday," Mike said. "At this gay happy hour at a bar in Chelsea. He was saying how much he liked you."

Mike was taking the long way down Edgemere Street. We passed by the Surf Lodge and rounded Fort Pond.

"Matt and I have gotten really close," I started. "I think..."

I could see Fort Pond through the trees. The flat glass water glistened blue and yellow. I didn't know what I thought.

"I think he's really awesome," I finally said.

"Yeah," Mike agreed as he flipped on the radio. "He's really great. I'm glad you two are friends."

There were nineteen people in the Hive that weekend. I was assigned to Bedroom 5, the smallest bedroom in the house, pressed between the larger basement bedroom and the Game Room. The air in Bedroom 5 breathed thin, and when the door was shut my sinuses closed up. At night, lying in one of the two twin beds, you could feel a cold aura tingle your flesh, as if a ghost had passed through.

That evening Ashley, Matt, and I were taking tequila shots in the kitchen. Someone had convinced us that tequila was an upper, so we guzzled back Milagro to jolt ourselves awake. It was only nine p.m., but Ashley was dead set on leaving by nine thirty. She wanted to get to Ruschmeyer's early. She had an intuitive feeling that something important was going to happen.

"Do you guys remember that guy I saw at the Sloppy Tuna over Memorial Day weekend? The one I locked eyes with on the upstairs deck? He was tall and wearing a water polo jacket?"

She had pretended he was no one, but I remembered. Ashley had stopped midsentence, her eyes shooting across the bar at the handsome guy in the windbreaker.

"I was on my way to Equinox on Tuesday and I saw him again. On Forty-Fourth and Lex. He was with a bunch of analysts; they were all in suits. They were probably on their way to lunch."

She was worked up from talking about him. Her fake eyelashes kept fluttering.

"Did you say anything to him?" Matt asked.

"God no. But we made eye contact again. He smiled at me. I know this sounds crazy, but I think I'm supposed to be with him. If someone is meant to be in my life, they keep circling back. I just have this feeling I'm going to run into him again."

"At Ruschmeyer's?" I asked. "Tonight? Do you know his name?"

"Not yet. But I'll find that out soon enough, too. I need to go straighten my hair. I already texted Henry to bring his cab in fifteen minutes. Anyone who wants to come with me can."

Just then Kirsten walked into the kitchen. She was wearing pearl earrings and her blond hair was swept up in a tight bun. She was dressed in the gaudy silk kimono from the master bedroom.

"Hello! Do you guys like my new outfit?" She swirled around and took a chug of wine from her clear plastic Hive cup.

"Tina!" Colby slammed his drink on the sideboard, rattling one of the twisted tubular glass candleholders. Next to them sat a big pewter bowl of lost items—BlackBerry chargers, hairbrushes, headphones, and nail polish. Tina was Kirsten's Montauk alter ego. When she got drunk, Tina came out in full force. Thus the Tina Juice.

"That kimono is fa-*shun*," said D.Lo.

"It looks like it's screaming at me," said Mike.

Kirsten kept dancing around, flipping her sashes and tossing Goldfish into her mouth.

Matt was laughing so hard he bent over and grabbed my arm. "This is the randomest house ever," he said. I agreed.

He told me about his week. He had just switched from the audit department to client strategy and the new workload was an adjustment. He'd worked until midnight three days that week.

"I don't mind the long hours," he said. "But it gets depressing eating Westville chicken at your desk every night."

On the upside, he loved his coworkers. His finance company was very gay friendly. They sponsored gay events and supported LGBT charities. It sounded like the opposite of Shane's situation.

"A lot of us have become good friends outside the office. But it's nice to have the Hive crew on the weekends."

"Are you coming for the Fourth of July?" I asked.

The returning housemates kept saying how the Fourth of July was the best weekend in Montauk. Mike and Colby were already planning a house party and a beach bonfire. I'd hoarded a few vacation days so I could head out on Wednesday night. I pictured Matt and myself drinking beers by the bonfire as snarls of driftwood crackled and burned.

"I'm missing it," Matt said. His voice was froggish, slightly affected. "I made plans to go to Provincetown back in, like, March."

"Oh. Well that'll be fun, I'm sure."

"Trust me, I'd much rather be in Montauk. I'm going with a group of people, including my ex-boyfriend."

I reached for the box of Goldfish. Tossed a few back.

"It'll be fine, I'm sure," he continued. "We're still friends. We met at work and dated off and on for a few months, but he was just coming out and still struggling with it." He paused, "I wish I were going to be in Montauk with you."

Kirsten and Colby processed back into the kitchen. This time Colby was wearing the kimono. Salt-N-Pepa's "Shoop" was playing and Colby started twerking around the kitchen, an embroidered blur of hot pink.

———————

Ashley and Mike got back to the house that night with a large cheese pizza from Pizza Village. They were the first ones home from the bar. They flicked on the deck lights and the bugs gathered around the glow. Ashley unsheathed two Marbs and they smoked on the back porch, listening to the sounds of the crickets. The rest of the house trickled in, some lingering for a slice or a nightcap before passing out on sand-strewn mattresses.

Colby was the last one home. He got back at three a.m. with two guys and a girl he had met at the Mem. The trio were college friends from Princeton and they were staying at the Beachcomber on the Old Montauk Highway. Colby had promised them a party.

The pizza was gone, but there was plenty of alcohol. They played a drinking game, Fuck the Dealer, in the kitchen. One of the guys, Joe, undid the top three buttons on his shirt and ran a hand through his cropped chest hair as he danced around the table. The other guy was Pete. He and Joe had played football together in college. The girl's name was Vanessa. Colby wouldn't remember any of this in the morning.

They took a round of tequila shots. Pete began to make out with Vanessa against the kitchen island. They were both tall and British and maybe models. Pete's hands reached around her back and grabbed her butt. She made space on the counter and he sat her against the ledge. Colby and Joe stepped into the living room to give them some privacy.

"Bro, thanks again for having us. And sorry about them," Joe said. They took a seat on the living room couch. It was dark, except for the light that leaked in from the kitchen.

"It's no problem, this house has seen way crazier, trust me."

"Oh yeah?" Joe rested his hand on Colby's thigh. "Like what?"

"You name it," Colby said.

Joe's tongue slid into Colby's mouth. He rested Colby against the couch and started to undress him.

"You told me you were straight," Colby said.

"I am."

Colby attracted people like this—big, masculine, confident guys and girls who were beautiful in an affluent way. As Colby took off Joe's shirt he could hear rhythmic moans from the kitchen. Pete and Vanessa were fucking against the counter.

———

The next morning, as the housemates coalesced, Pete, who boasted flowing hair and a Crest Whitestrips smile, earned the nickname One Direction. It was also revealed that Joe had nipple rings. The trio had vanished before most of the house woke up.

"Colby!" Kirsten tossed a pillow at him from across the living room. "You cannot date someone with nipple rings!"

"Who said anything about date?"

"What if you'd accidentally ripped one out?" Mike said. "What if his nipple had fallen off on our couch?"

We starfished across the living room in various states of ruin. I lay on my back, limbs sinking into the shag carpet, counting the knots on the ceiling. We called these sessions Morning Therapy. The girls came down in men's boxers and oversize T-shirts as the guys brushed their teeth in the kitchen sink. Hungover, exhausted, arms smeared with bar stamps, we were defenseless and unvarnished in a decidedly collective way.

Matt was sprawled out next to me in his blue Lululemon shirt. "I think I left my credit card at the Point."

I writhed on the ground. "I think I left a horcrux."

"You kill me," he said, laughing.

"We'll go into town and gather them both today."

We curled on the couches and chairs and laughed until our abs hurt. We fought to get a word in. Someone always came through with the perfect line. In the fizzy terrain between drunk and hungover, we sought comfort in physical proximity. But most of all we sought reassurance. We wanted to know we hadn't done anything too embarrassing. That we weren't that bad. That honestly, we were fine.

For the first time since the car accident I felt swaddled and safe. I felt protected in a way I hadn't since childhood.

"I'm so hungover," Kirsten moaned. "I can't do this. I need to go back to bed forever."

Colby stood over her, togged in his workout gear. "Girl, if

Britney can get through 2007, you can get through this day. Grab yourself some Tina Juice and make a glass for your father."

I listened to the sounds of recovery. The stream of the tap. The shake of an Advil bottle. The eye-opening crack of a cold Bud Light. Cars came and went, taking orders for the Bake Shoppe or Herb's Market or Jack's Stir Brew Coffee in Amagansett.

The screen door slid open, sweeping in a cool pine breeze. Ashley entered in a sports bra and yoga pants, body glistening with sweat. She had already gone for a five-mile run.

Our Morning Therapy sessions harkened back to high school, when my parents and I would return from Sunday Mass to find my friends Bryan and Brett playing Nintendo in our living room. You didn't have to knock at our house, you could just walk in—even, my friends figured out, when the Glynns weren't home.

"We just called Annie. She's on her way," Brett would say, without looking up from *Mario Kart*. "Grab a controller. You can be Yoshi."

My parents loved it—the familiarity, the liberation, the way our friend group took on the hues of a family. Our house became the hang-out house, the place where we'd go when we didn't have a plan.

As I grew older, I assumed those days were behind me—the carefree intimacy of profusion. The sense of living life as a group. But the Hive, by definition, was communal. We existed as one unit, for better or worse.

We got to the beach around eleven and set up camp at our spot beyond the volleyball nets. I was sitting in a beach chair next to a housemate I hadn't met before. Her name was Kelsey O'Brian, and everyone called her by her full name. She had straight blond hair and flawless pale skin. I could tell already that she was quick-witted and vulgar. Due to the rotating schedule, our weekends hadn't previously overlapped. But within our first fifteen minutes on the beach, she had already made multiple jokes about Daisy Buchanan's asshole. I was on board.

"Oh my GOD!" Kelsey shouted. She was clutching her phone with both hands, face twisted with panic.

"What's happening?" I asked.

"Fucking Christ!"

"What is it?" Mike asked.

Everyone turned to watch her. She was bent over laughing, freckled hands covering her face.

"Guys, I..." She was laughing so hard she was wheezing. Finally she composed herself enough to finish. "My phone just emailed porn to my ex-boyfriend's mom."

For a beat the entire group went silent. Then we erupted into laughter.

"My email says, get this: 'Dearest, I found something I thought you would like. Check out these pics of me and my friends.' The link is of two chicks riding a double-sided dildo."

We were doubled over on our chairs and beach blankets. Kelsey, like me, was a new house member. The Hive seemed to attract these unfiltered extroverts. People who weren't afraid to wave their freak flags.

"I haven't seen or spoken to this woman in five years."

"Did it send to anyone else?" Mike asked. "Or did it, like, single out your ex's mom?"

Kelsey scrolled through her sent items. "Oh no!" She clicked through another email. "It sent a weight loss program to my obese college English professor!"

Kelsey was staring at her phone in abject horror, clicking on links between sips of Bud Light. She went silent for a minute, her fingers tapping out a message across her touch screen. For the rest of the morning she remained locked in a battle with a Taiwanese bot, attempting to wrest back control of her email account. By lunchtime she had prevailed.

After a swim I was flipping through an issue of *Vanity Fair*. The pages were stiff and salt-battered, mixed with water droplets and grains of sand. They crinkled when I turned them. Every few minutes I'd look up from the article about Pippa Middleton to check the crowd at the Sloppy Tuna. Once the deck started to look like it might collapse, that was our cue to head over.

Approaching the entrance, I was surprised to see a line. Most of the people waiting between the switchback ropes wore bathing suits and flip-flops, but some were teased up in full-fledged club gear. Chests burst through fitted graphic tees. High heels stabbed into the sun-softened blacktop. The dichotomy reflected the general vibe of Montauk that summer. The beachgoer and the scene seeker. To the locals they were probably one and the same, I thought, as Ashley kissed the bouncer and ushered us through the line.

We paired off. Colby with Kirsten. D.Lo with Perrie. Ashley with Mike. Me with Matt. If you ordered a Transfusion but swapped the ginger ale for seltzer, it technically became a vodka soda with a splash of grape juice. This drink was four dollars cheaper, plus it tasted better. I got Matt's first round and he got my second. We found my college friends and Tribeca neighbors, Caroline and Charlotte, drinking rum punches on the deck.

"Where are your shoes?" asked Matt.

"Shoes?" Caroline looked at Charlotte. "We don't use those things."

"Isn't there a rule?" I asked.

"Of course there is. But not for us."

Matt looking on approvingly. "I'm sticking with you guys."

I got in line for the bathroom. The urinals were speckled with sand and wads of gum. EDM music was muffled by the swinging doors. As I washed my hands, breathing in the caustic scent of piss, I kept my head down, avoiding the mirror. Sometimes the sight of my reflection kicked up a feeling of disappointment so intense that it overshadowed any excitement around me. One glance could sink me into a pool of dread. I'd inspect my reflection and ask myself the same question over and over. *How is this me?*

I exited the bathroom just as the women's room door was swinging open. I couldn't help but peer in. Ashley was standing in front of the mirror, her big pebbled bag resting by the sink. Her head was cocked at an unnatural angle. Eyes trained forward. It took me a moment to register what I was seeing. She was running her hair through a hot metal clamp, then combing it out with her hands. The movement carried a manic energy, a compulsive freneticism I found both fascinating and unsettling. That she had brought her hair straightener to the beach, that she had chosen to use it at the Sloppy Tuna. These facts suddenly seemed to inform all the others.

Upstairs Colby was posing for a photo with Perrie. Behind them the ocean extended as far as the eye could see, the waves crashing in wild curls of cerulean. D.Lo snapped a few pics and handed the phone back to Perrie. She inspected the snapshots and selected the best one for Instagram. She uploaded the photo, applied a filter, and posted.

It was three p.m. and Colby was already very drunk. He was sloshing around his second rum punch and some of it had spilled on his shorts, though his dirty-blond hair was still perfectly swept to the side. He grabbed the phone from Perrie's hands and inspected the post. His brows knitted together. He trapped Perrie's arm.

"Take it down."

"What? No way! It's so cute!"

"I look fat. Take it down."

"Oh, please. You look so handsome. It's such a great pic of us."

"Fine. If you don't take it down I will." Colby seized her phone and shark-finned across the deck.

"Colby!" Perrie caught up to him and attempted to pry the phone from his hands. "Colby, give it back, I'm serious!"

Colby swung his elbow so violently that Perrie jumped back. He clicked delete and handed the phone back to her. "Don't ever embarrass me like that again."

"Colby, you're being insane. That was a perfectly fine pho—"

"Stop being a fucking BITCH, Perrie."

"Colby—"

"Get the fuck away from me. I'm serious. The only reason

you're in the house is because of me. No one else even likes you."

Perrie's eyes started to well up. She took her phone back and placed it in her bag. Matt and I watched her run down the stairs.

Something was wrong with Colby. His eyes were sunken. His cherubic face hung slack. He was working twelve, fourteen, sixteen hours a day. He was not eating well or exercising. He had told me once, on a drive back to the city, that his uncle had died of a heart attack at forty-three. He was worried he was driving himself to the same fate.

Over the past month Colby and I had grown close—he'd told me I was his new favorite housemate—but I always treated our exchanges with hypervigilance, afraid at every turn I'd set off some invisible trip wire. I wasn't yet sure if he was always like this, or if something bigger was going on.

———

Colby went home, and Perrie managed to shrug things off. We drove to Cyril's fish shack, drank banana drinks in the gravel parking lot, and returned to the Hive. On the way home I asked Shane to let me off at Gurney's. I needed an iced coffee, and the seaside hotel had a small café.

The hours of five to nine were reserved for triage. Drunk and sun-crisped, we hovered near the air vents, stuck our faces in the thick coolant of the freezer. We changed into T-shirts and tanks from local shops like Air + Speed, Wampum, and Whalebone—clothes designed for comfort. Some took showers, some reached for beers. Mike had a Ziploc bag filled with pills, his "trail mix." The blue ones were Adderall. He'd place them on our housemates' outstretched tongues like wafers of holy communion.

Some people cobbled together meals—peanut butter and white bread, hot dogs and eggs, half a bag of soggy potato chips. I had learned early on that my panacea was caffeine. At Gurney's I slid a few soaked bills across the counter and returned to the Hive with my iced coffee in tow.

Night fell and it was my turn to shower. It was an unspoken rule that the girls showered in the blue bathroom upstairs. Mike and Colby, who were particular about their bathrooms, also showered upstairs. Everyone else showered down.

I turned on the water and stepped into the beige overlay tub. My skin was burned, and the warm water seemed to release the heat I'd absorbed throughout the day. Showering was the only time in Montauk when I was truly alone with my thoughts. Even then people would sometimes come in to use the bathroom. As the water streamed down my back I felt an unfamiliar sense of totality. A sweep of emotion, so saturated and confounding it froze me to the tub. I was overwhelmed by the Hive's abundance—the way it gave my weeks shape and momentum. Not quite purpose, but direction. And I feared what would happen when it went away.

I fought in vain to keep the dark thoughts at bay. You are alone, you will always be alone, you are destined to die that way. Everybody wants to be your friend, but no one wants to truly get close to you because if they did, they would see that at your core, you are entirely, inviolately, perfectly unlovable. Individually your physical features are benign. On others they'd even be attractive. But the coalescence of those features has created a force field so repellent that no one will ever love you.

I got out of the shower and stood facing the mirror. I leaned against the sink, dripping naked on the shaggy brown bath mat that lay across the linoleum like a square of bear fur. I was trying to breathe. Trying to psych myself up. Trying to will everything to be okay. I streaked my hand across the mirror and stared at my reflection through the steam. *You got this*, I kept telling myself. *You got this. You're awesome. You're with your friends. You're going to have fun.* I stared into my eyes and forced myself to smile.

Back in the kitchen, everyone glowed a healthy crimson. Drunk from Cyril's, Timmy donned a pair of Ashley's wedges. He dropped his shoulders, twisted his hips, the shoes sliding along the linoleum floor. Kelsey O'Brian twerked up against him, the two of them dipping and grinding like mating butterflies. The night had started.

Matt was testing the limits of my iPod, requesting songs he thought I was missing. I played "Countdown" by Beyoncé and Christina Aguilera's "Dirrty." I played "Hold On" by Wilson Phillips. Everyone in the house began to sing along.

"What about Garth Brooks?" he asked.

Beyond a few down-home frat songs and Johnny Cash, I was never a big country fan. I told him I had "Standing Outside the Fire." But that was it.

"John. I'm appalled!"

He went to the living room and returned holding Shane's L.L.Bean beach tote. He grabbed my hand.

"Come with me."

I followed him through the back porch and onto the vast split-level deck, dimly aware of the beguiling feeling gathering in my chest. To our right, at shoulder level, lay the garage roof. It was low-pitched and climbable, the perfect angle for stargazing. Matt climbed up, his pink shorts flaring in the dark. The indoor music gave way to night sounds—crickets and owls, wind through trees.

"It's so peaceful out here," he said. "I need a break from inside."

He arranged the portable speakers on a brown beach blanket and plugged in his iPhone. He turned to me, eyes raised.

"Aren't you coming up?"

I pressed my palms to the roof, the shingles coarse like sandpaper, the sharpness digging into my elbows and knees.

"I have to pick the perfect song," he said. "Just like you always do."

"The pressure's on."

I lay next to him but kept my eyes trained on the hillside.

"How do you do it?" he asked. "How do you play the exact right song at the exact right time?" His hand grazed my wrist for a fleeting moment, a touch so light it could have been an accident, a mistake. It redirected my gaze. He was looking right at me.

"I don't know. You just kinda read the crowd and anticipate what they want."

"Okay, I'm gonna do that now, but for you."

He pressed play on a Rihanna song, "Do Ya Thang." I had never heard it before, but I liked it immediately. The melody felt serene and adolescent, dipped in hues of pink and purple. Like an eighties pop song infused with hip-hop beats. The lyrics spoke of an expansive type of coupledom, a lover who gives her partner the freedom to embrace his true nature. It was somehow catchy and soothing.

We lay on the blanket and gazed up. The stars draped the sky, as big and low as lanterns.

"Don't you wish we got stars like this in the city?" His hand touched my arm again, and lingered.

He hit play on a Garth Brooks song I'd never heard before. Garth was his favorite artist. Matt had written his college essay about "The Dance."

"'Our lives are better left to chance. I could have missed the pain, but I'd have had to miss the dance.'"

"The dance is always worth it, right? Have you ever seen him live?"

"No. He basically stopped performing. If he ever goes on tour I'll see every one of his shows. I'll like, quit my job and follow him like a Phish fan."

"Why do you like him so much?" I asked.

"He reminds me of growing up. He was my dad's favorite, too. I used to lock myself in my room and listen to him. A lot of his songs are really sad."

I thought back to my high school experience—the basement pregames, the endless drives, the secret bonfires by the Connecticut River. We weren't the good kids, but we weren't the bad ones. We got A's and B's in honors courses. We played sports. We volunteered at Special Olympics events and diabetes walkathons.

I'd felt everything so deeply back then. The comforting knots of friendship. The girl I thought I loved. The heartache I'd felt was real and bottomless but seemed self-inflicted in hindsight. What did I have to compare?

"What made you sad?" I asked. We were lying close together. Our bodies were almost touching, but not. Everything felt accelerated, dangerous, intensified, shot through with light against dark. Our hands and legs kept touching and this time I did not flinch.

"It was weird. I loved high school and was happy. I had a lot of friends and got good grades. But I was also really sad at the same time. I was starting to figure out I was gay. And the weird thing was, I had nothing to fear. I had this great family. But when you're from a family that genuinely gets along, you never want to disappoint them or have them worry about you."

"The stakes feel higher," I said, picking up his thought, "because you care so much. It's the same with my family."

"You never want to be a burden. Not that being gay is a burden. But back then the world seemed less hospitable toward gay people. I didn't want my family to worry about me facing isolation or ridicule or anything. I wanted to protect them. But I was living a lie and it was only getting worse."

"That's where Garth came in?"

"Haha. Yup."

We lay there, clicking through songs, talking about our childhoods, our families, our darker moments, our hopes. It felt as if he were verbalizing my thoughts, and I his, that our perspectives, our words and feelings, were indistinguishable. I imagined that this was what birth was like, if one could experience it cognitively—the torturous slipstream of untested senses, the prising open of chambers and vessels, the instability of air, the terrifying power of proximity, vision, and incidental touch. I had never felt more immediately pinned to the present. Yet every moment also grasped at the future, stretching toward the promise of a new and expansive life. I saw my future—our future, together—as an infinite unfurling moment transmogrified into scenes domestic, quotidian, and grandiose. A car ride where we held hands. A mudroom filled with kids' soccer cleats. A morning spent in blankets as the windows swirled with snow. These visions nested in each moment like hard, smooth pearls.

The stars crystallized above us. More and more appeared. Time sped up, slowed down, and dissolved altogether. Three hours had passed with us on the roof, and I didn't care what anyone inside was thinking. Every other thought faded to mist. I sensed my old life dematerializing, my soul reconstituting itself around him. I had never felt more connected to another human. My heart was opening and breaking all at once.

That night, on the roof, Matt became the organizing principle of my world.

Kirsten was hunting for Stefano. He had posted a photo from Zum Schneider, a German beer hall by the Mem that served ale in glass steins. She did a lap through the bar with Perrie, holding her hand, avoiding gazes, driven by a singular purpose. She refused to text Stefano. She would not ask him where he was.

When it was clear that he was not there, they returned to the Point, where the rest of us were downing shots of Fireball.

Perrie saw through Kirsten's vacant smile. "Fuck Stefano. Go find the tallest tree in the bar and climb him. Look, Kirsten, look. There are the Tots."

A group of guys were clustered at the back of the bar. They had met the Hive girls one weekend in early June, sharing watermelon drinks from their glass pitcher at Ruschmeyer's. They were fresh out of college—twenty-two and twenty-three. They barreled around Montauk like a litter of golden retrievers. Their beer cans always seemed to open with explosions of foam.

Nick was tall, six foot five, in a gingham shirt and Rainbow sandals. He had been pursuing Kirsten for almost a month, but she had rebuffed his advances. She was still hung up on Stefano. She didn't have the room for him.

Objectively, Kirsten was perhaps the most attractive girl in the house. Her large, almond-shaped eyes and bee-stung lips evoked a delicate, avian beauty, a mesmeric power akin to the sand art of Tibetan monks—colorful and exacting, precarious, transitory. She had been broken many times.

As Kirsten grew increasingly unmoored, her instability infected her self-image. She would never return to the abyss she'd occupied in college, but she was deeply unhappy with her body that summer. She covered herself with men's clothes. Plaid button-downs half tucked into old Abercrombie jeans she fashioned into cut-offs. She wore a leather belt her dad had made in the seventies. In reality, she was five foot seven, 126 pounds. But Stefano's vicissitudes only amplified her insecurities.

When Nick Tot approached her that night, she decided to let him.

Chapter Thirteen

On Monday, July 1, Mike was panicking. The Fourth of July was the busiest holiday in Montauk. Twenty-seven people were scheduled to stay at the Hive.

Ashley called him from the Old Montauk Highway. She had stayed out the night before—a Surf Lodge Sunday. She reported that both the Hive toilets were broken. Mike assured her it was not her fault. The plumbing was not designed for such high-volume traffic. It was bound to give out eventually.

Mike sat cross-legged on his couch in Stuytown. His laptop was cradled between his thighs. He called the owner and left a voicemail. Then he opened his email. He had two hours to follow up with his beta users before his shift began at SoulCycle.

Since launching his company Mike had worked from home. He kept his important documents in a mahogany breakfront—an antique table Shane had procured. To Shane, Stuytown was just a sprawling repetition of redbrick high-rises, a dry run before their real apartment. But for Mike it carried hints of romance. His grandparents had lived in Stuytown for a time. His mother had lived there as a newborn. When Mike launched his company, the apartment became his headquarters. But for Shane it felt like an extension of dorm life. Their lease was up at the end of August, and Shane was counting down the days.

Shane didn't see the world the way Mike did. Shane was miserable. His antidepressants weren't working. He resented Mike for his failed start-up and his false promises of financial security. Mike detested Shane's obsession with material things. In public they wore a veil of harmony, but that summer the seams of their tattered relationship were beginning to show. They hadn't had sex in months.

The owner called back. A plumber was booked for Tuesday, the earliest available appointment. Mike thanked her, and asked that she keep him updated. He ran a hand through his red hair. The first housemates were supposed to arrive on Wednesday afternoon, and not all the Hivers were low-maintenance. Everyone had an opinion about room assignments, divisions of labor, and the allocation of house funds. Broken toilets would be, at best, a point of contention. For Mike, the Hive was the one sphere in his life where he had total control. When something went wrong he felt it was his fault.

Adding to his anxiety was the fact that he had invited a guest. His name was Parker. He was what Colby called a "stray cat." Mike had met him at an "Out in Finance" happy hour, then they ran into each other again at SoulCycle. Parker was new to the city and had never been to Montauk.

Mike refilled his coffee. Parker's toothy smile and easy laugh conveyed to him something virtuous. Mike was drawn to him. He didn't quite know why. Maybe it was Parker's loneliness. Mike felt an urge to take him in, to protect him.

As a failsafe, Mike contacted Callahead and reserved a portable toilet. The representative emailed him back almost instantly. She seemed truly dedicated to the disposal of human shit. He knew the Hive was in good hands.

———————————

That Monday morning on my walk to the 6 train, I said a prayer to my grandmother. Something was happening to me. Something physical. My muscles were weak. My hands grew shaky. When I took a deep breath, my rib cage compressed, and everything around me felt precarious and blurry. I walked down Duane Street, passing West Broadway. I carried my sneakers in a worn gym bag, the straps constantly threatening to come undone. *Kicki,* I prayed, *I don't know what I need. But please help me.*

A random song came on my iPod and my eyes grew unexpectedly dewy. I felt wholly disarmed, overwhelmed by the loneliness and beauty of the world. I felt everything at once. Excitement. Anxiety. A mix of elation and terror that left me nauseous.

I knew what this was. I knew it by name. I'd thought I had experienced it before, but I hadn't—at least not in such a rich swirl of colors and tones, shades and nuances. Not with the same depth and intensity. Not in its true form. This was what my parents talked about.

I was falling for someone.

That someone was a guy, not a girl.

I was so unbalanced, I could barely breathe. These feelings—of love, infatuation, blinding euphoria—were entirely foreign to me. I had always anticipated they'd come attached to a woman. I understood that sexuality wasn't always fixed, and the events at my Christmas party—a shared ice luge, Fred's affirmations—had already made me think about my own capacity for same-sex attraction. But that encounter had been soaked in Fireball. My feelings for Matt, however, were concrete and experiential. I was falling for him and I didn't know what it meant. All I knew was what I felt: a kind of giddy, queasy, terrifying downrush that framed all my waking thoughts.

I crossed Church Street, passing the firehouse, my mind aflame. I thought about Matt. Then I thought about Matt. Then I thought about Matt. I had never felt this way before. At twenty-seven, I was experiencing my first true crush.

I was so relieved I could cry.

I spent a distracted day at work attempting to create marketing materials for a memoir called *The Promise of a Pencil*. I was so consumed, so enamored I thought I would detonate. I needed to talk to someone, but the notion left me paralyzed. I was unsure of who to confide in, which of my friends would be least likely to judge.

Mike seemed like a logical confidant, but I was afraid of his reaction. The rational part of me believed he'd validate me. He might even be thrilled. But his experience had been much different than mine. He had always known he was gay, and he'd never had relationships with girls. I didn't even know if Matt represented a one-off, or a new way of being in the world. When Mike appeared in my Gchat list, I hovered the cursor over his name. I opened a blank chat window, then closed it. I needed to gather the courage—and the vocabulary—to explain.

———————

Of all the girls in the Hive, I found D.Lo the most intimidating. Along with Mike and Colby, she had founded the Hive the summer before. Though her name was no longer on the lease, she still exerted her influence in the Hive's collective decisions. She was not fragile like some of the other people in the house. She was the most effortlessly cool. She spoke in calm assertions. Her gaze was cold, luminous, and resistant to interpretation.

D.Lo lived in Murray Hill, a rowdy neighborhood just below Midtown. Her apartment was corralled by neon sports bars and endless packs of roving bros. "Murray Thrill," as she called it, was anything but. She no longer found excitement in yelling into the ears of former lacrosse players at two o'clock in the morning.

Montauk, for D.Lo, was a space for real discourse. She spent long afternoons with Matt walking from Hither Hills to Ditch Plains, delving into life's greatest mysteries. Relationships, family, spirituality, the transcendent power of art and song. These were the types of conversations she had been craving. This was the kind of depth her city life lacked. Like many of us, D.Lo yearned for love but found sustenance in friendship. She was happier when her gaze shifted toward the Hive.

D.Lo was twenty-six, blond, tall, attractive, confident, debt-free, and the owner of a three-thousand-dollar handbag. She was also lovelorn, adrift, confused and hopeless. She had not had a meaningful relationship in over a year, and the self-imposed pressure of finding a match had peaked that spring. That week, as she packed her Montauk bag, she envisioned a future life animated by work promotions, travel, time spent with family. A boyfriend, a partner, no longer seemed tenable. She was destined to be single. As she packed her bag for Montauk, she decided she was done with guys.

———————

That night I went to Reade Street Pub with my roommates. In the past month I had seen little of them. Evan had bought into the share house but had only gone out once. Chauvin had been traveling for weddings and bachelor parties. They were both planning to spend the Fourth of July in Montauk—Evan and his girlfriend at the Hive, Chauvin and his girlfriend at the Montauk Blue Hotel. I was anxious about how the two circles would mix. Other college friends would be joining them, including the girls, our Tribeca neighbors, who were in their own share house off West Lake Drive.

Reade Street Pub was a brick-wall dive with low coffered ceilings. A few regulars were drinking silently in the dull liquescent light. The bartender drew us cold pints of beer. On the countertop sat a schoolhouse globe. The three of us had come up with a drinking game that utilized it. One person picked an obscure country and another had five seconds to find it. We cradled the globe, spinning it through our fingers.

"Find...Burkina Faso!"

"...Suriname!"

"...Bhutan!"

Chauvin had seen photos of our housemates on social media. He knew the girls were very attractive.

"Are all of them single?"

My flesh tightened. I knew where this thread would lead.

"Most of them, yep."

"Are you going for any of them?"

The question came from a place of heartfelt interest, but it clenched me like a bear trap. Chauvin and Evan were like brothers to me. I told them everything. But the Matt situation was way too much. It would change things. The idea of such a paradigm shift terrified me. I wanted us all to be the same.

"Nah," I said.

"What about that girl Kirsten? She's super hot," said Evan.

"Kirsten's great."

"You should go for it."

"Nah. She's outta my league."

I grabbed the teal globe, its raised topography like Braille beneath my fingers. Hanging pendant lights reflected off the plastic. I spun the world on its axis until the continents melded into a color-streaked blur. The Fourth of July was a few days away.

Chapter Fourteen

On Wednesday, July 3, I went home to Massachusetts. I had seven days off and planned to borrow my mom's car. I would spend the weekend in Montauk, then drive to the Connecticut shore to meet my parents. I was cutting into family time to go to the Hive.

My parents were growing concerned about my time in Montauk. To them the Hamptons represented unchecked hedonism, and my text messages and calls, which often came on Sundays when I was at my most vulnerable, didn't exactly assuage their fears. They chalked up my anxiety to alcohol, and while I attempted to stay their worries, I provided little in the way of a counternarrative. Occasionally, via text, I made oblique references to heartsickness. But both my parents were entirely convinced that I would find the right girl soon enough.

"Listen to me, Johnny," my mom said as she reheated her Dunkin' Donuts coffee in the microwave. "I worry about everything. But the one thing I'm not worried about is you finding love. It'll happen sooner than you think."

It was easier for me to exist in the vacuum of my emotions than to think about their broader implications. I was less concerned with how my same-sex feelings might impact my family, and more concerned about coping with my crush. For that I needed to rely on Mike's help.

As terrified as I was to verbalize my attraction, I was confident that Mike was the one friend I could trust. I was determined to talk to him that weekend. The terrible euphoria was growing too strong. I was so stuck in my head, I felt trapped. I needed to sort through my feelings out loud. I wanted to ask Mike a million questions. I wanted to draw a map of my heart and hold it up to him and have him help me figure out where the fuck I was.

I rose with the sun in my childhood bedroom. Amber light washed the empty streets of our neighborhood. I drove an hour and a half to New London and cruised onto the Cross Sound Ferry before nine thirty, finding a sunny spot on the outside deck to read Stephen King's *Joyland*. At Orient Point, my chest thrummed with excitement. I reached the drop-off and ferried to Shelter Island, then ferried again to Sag Harbor. By Amagansett the crowds were out. American flags fluttered from the light posts. "The Stars and Stripes Forever" echoed from an antique car.

The Hive was ringing with a sunstruck energy. I hugged Ashley and Colby, kissed Kirsten on the cheek, yelled to the finance bros, who were blasting country music on the deck. Perrie wore American flag sunglasses, her arms belted in glow sticks. I dropped my bag in the basement and changed into my bathing suit.

I found Mike in the kitchen pouring vodka into a plastic jug. He was ecstatic to report that the toilets had been fixed just in time.

Kirsten had been walking around the house, yelling, in a nod to *Mean Girls*, "You can't shit with us."

He outlined our plans for the day. Beach, Tuna, Cyril's, then a VIP room at the Memory Motel.

"Ashley and I talked to the owner," he explained. "They're converting two bedrooms into a private space, giving us three bottles, a case of Red Bull, and unlimited beer. Thirty dollars a head. The house will cover the rest. We automatically get to cut the line. They've never done anything like this before."

He glugged Fresca into the vodka jug and poured in a full can of Coors Light. Then he added three fingers of Milagro tequila.

"What is that?" I asked.

"Rocket Fuel. For the beach."

"Jesus."

"Just wait. This is the craziest day of the year. Kirsten's pregaming with Windex."

We both started laughing. Back in college we used to pose with household cleaners and pretend to drink them. We'd take pictures and send them to our parents. *Having a blast in college. Wholesome coed fun!*

I sat on the counter as Mike capped the jug. We were the only two in the kitchen.

"Mikey, I've got something I need to talk through with you."

His face narrowed. "Everything okay?"

I clenched my teeth, tried to channel a strength I knew I lacked.

"Yeah, everything's fine. I. I'm just going through something confusing and need your help."

"Yeah, bud. Of course. What's going on?"

I felt a sudden force at my back. I flew off the kitchen island, onto the floor. Someone had shoved me.

I turned to see Shane swaying on the laminate. He was dressed in a tank top and a neon bathing suit. His eyes were dull.

"Ya trashy, where's ya trailer."

I looked him up and down. In his hands were a glass pipe and a small bag of weed. I could smell liquor coming from his pores.

"He's in full-on bitch mode," Mike said.

"I can see that."

"Oh, you can?" Shane slurred. "You can see that. Good for fucking you." I couldn't tell if he was mimicking bro talk or if he was truly being combative. He roved across the counter, snagging a fistful of Doritos. "The toilets are fixed," he added. "Plumber came. You're welcome."

D.Lo came into the kitchen in a pink Triangl bathing suit. She was looking down at her phone.

"Just got a text from Matt," she announced. "He overslept for his ferry to P-town. Their trip is already a shitshow."

"I don't know why he's going to that dump in the first place," Shane drolled. "Have fun getting syphilis."

D.Lo eyed Shane with disapproval.

"Tell him to forget Provincetown and come to the Hive!" Mike said.

"Ha, I know. I'm trying. Has anyone seen my Vera Bradley tote? It's light green."

"I think it's in the Rover," Mike said.

"You mean the Hamptons Honda," Shane joked.

I imagined Matt abandoning his plans, arriving at Montauk by nightfall. I knew such a trek was not in the cards, but the mere thought brought me comfort. I was already looking forward to the next time we'd be back at the Hive together.

We reached Sloppy Tuna Beach by twelve thirty. I had never seen Montauk so crowded. Through the open back window of the Rover I watched the stream of surfers, fishermen, and city dwellers. We parked at St. Therese of Lisieux, a Catholic church four blocks from the sea.

The beach had the jostled spirit of a carnival. We arranged our chairs in a horseshoe, but everyone was standing and mingling. Red Solo cups filled with Mike's Rocket Fuel. The waves were big and we swam out past where they broke so we could wade, float, and chat. Next to our camp a girl in a string bikini was snorting cocaine off a music speaker. Two kids from the Slide House entertained us with acro-yoga, one floating swanlike across the other's feet. A girl moved up and down the coast while spinning a hula hoop along her waist. In the crush of people, cell phones ceased to work.

Kirsten came up to me. I was holding the bottle of Rocket Fuel, entranced by Ashley, who was playing Kadima with Tyler.

"There are the Tots," Kristen said, nodding discreetly toward the bro pack setting up camp next to us. "Gimme somma dat Tina Juice."

Kirsten had been flitting between her thirty-eight-year-old Stefano, and her twenty-three-year-old infatuation, Nick Tot.

"Amazing what a difference fifteen years can make," she said.

I drank a cup of Rocket Fuel, then switched to beer, attempting to quell my rising anxiety. My college friends were planning to meet us on the beach, and I continued to worry about how they'd coexist with the Hive. More precisely, I wondered how it would all look to them—me relaxed among fifteen drunk gay guys, seemingly uncompelled by the attractive girls around me. Since the rooftop, I had total clarity about my feelings toward Matt. But I had no idea where that placed me categorically.

A tremor of fear rippled through me. If my straight friends found out, despite their liberal outlook, it might shift our friendships in subtle but irretrievable ways. I'd never feel at ease with them again, and vice versa.

I finished off my beer and grabbed another. I tried to remind myself that my feelings for Matt were bottled up and safe. They existed in my mind alone. But they weren't safe; they were tremendously volatile, and I had absolutely no idea how to negotiate them. For the next twenty minutes I lay in the sand, my mind weighted like an unlit bomb.

I sought out Mike down by the water. He was chatting with D.Lo. I was messy and panicked, and he felt like my life raft.

"Did you hear about this new sober dance party thing?" he was saying. "You go on your lunch break, dance for an hour with your coworkers, then go back to work. They're doing it at Marquee."

"I'd rather eat a salad at my desk alone," D.Lo said as she shackled her hair into a ponytail. "I'm going in the water. You boys care to join?"

Mike said no, he refused to go swimming until August. I declined.

We watched D.Lo walk slowly into the waves, clutching her chest and bracing against the surf. Mike turned to me. "How ya doing, Johnny Drama?"

"I'm okay. Have you seen our BC friends? I think they're on the way."

"Yeah. So is my friend Parker. I'm getting shitty service, though. I don't want to miss him."

"Look, Mikey, I need to talk to you about something."

"Ugh, I know—I'm sorry. Tyler wasn't supposed to be in your room. He decided to come out last night and I didn't know where to sleep him. I'll tell him he's on the couch tonight."

"No, it's not that."

"Oh. Then what's up?"

He had no clue. This life pivot. This total shift in my reality. Was it really undetectable to the outside world?

"Oh, look! Here comes Parker! Yo, Parker!"

I spotted a pale kid trudging along the dune line. He was shirtless, his chest concave. He was eyeing the beach the way a child might scrutinize a roller coaster—with fear, excitement, and a willful mustering of courage.

"John, this is my buddy Parker," Mike introduced. "He's staying at the Hive this weekend."

Parker had a youthful face and a receding hairline. The effect was that of a religious painting.

"Hey, man, nice to meet you," I said. "First time to Montauk?"

"Yeah!" he replied, dropping his backpack. "This is crazy! There are people over there playing beer pong in a giant sand pit. Is it always like this?"

Mike scanned the beach. "Honestly? I've been coming out for years and I've never seen it this crowded. Here." He handed Parker the Coors Light he'd just grabbed for himself. "You need to catch up."

Parker cracked the stay tab and the beer exploded in his face. He wiped foam from his eyes and cheeks, a streak from his chest. I felt bad. Two minutes in and he was already covered in beer.

Mike tried to apologize, but Parker was smiling. "I can't think of a more fitting way to kick off the weekend," he said, his gaze fixed on Mike, his smile cutting through everything.

I listened as Mike brought Parker up to speed. It was a busy day across the Hamptons. There was talk of a house party at an East Hampton estate; guests would be given fine cigars and custom suiting. In Water Mill a nonprofit was throwing a poolside benefit, complete with celebrity guests and Bootlegger vodka. Closer by, the Montauk Yacht Club was hosting Shark Attack, an annual party aglow with neon, inflatables, and designer drugs.

"I got my ticket yesterday," Parker said. "Are you guys going?" I had been on the Shark Attack emails, but hadn't purchased a ticket. It didn't seem like my scene. Mike wasn't going either.

"It's nuts," Mike warned. "Someone died last year. If you go, be careful."

By the time my BC friends arrived my anxiety had dissipated. I was drunk and happier, flushed from the sun. Alcohol and the profusion of the Hive were their own kind of catharsis. I introduced my BC friends to some of our housemates, but it was Ashley who caught their attention. She had just emerged from the ocean and was manically spraying her hair with detangler.

"Oh my God, you guys. You won't believe this." I was standing with my two roommates, their girlfriends, and Mike. Ashley had approached without introduction. "The Sloppy Tuna asked me to be in a bikini contest Saturday. If I do it I get free drinks all weekend. And two free bathing suits."

"No way!" Mike said. "Are you gonna do it?"

"I don't know. I feel like I'd be so awkward!" She turned to

Evan's girlfriend, Lizzie, whom she had never met. "What do you think?"

"Hell." Lizzie looked her up and down. "If I looked like you I'd do it in a second."

"Oh stop, I'm so fat right now, all I did last week was eat ice cream. I'd only do it for the free drinks. I could hand them off to all of you."

"I say do it!" chimed in Amelia, Chauvin's girlfriend. "We'll cheer you on."

"You guys are the sweetest. I'm Ashley, by the way. You all went to BC with these two, right?" She grabbed Lizzie's beach cover-up. "That's the cutest tunic."

"Sale at Cynthia Rowley," Lizzie said.

"Oh my God I love her." She turned to Amelia. "You both look so beautiful. I wish I had gone to BC. You guys are all such good friends to each other."

Like that she disappeared into another game of Kadima, another game of football, an endless swirl of sports and activities. Only in motion could Ashley's mind truly rest.

Thunderous waves smashed the sand, whisking me back to a windy day at Hawk's Nest Beach. When I was little, my cousin Jay and I received a gift from our aunt Momo, a toy soldier attached to a parachute of cellophane. For a week we brought the soldier to the beach with us every day, tossing him through the sky and watching, in wonder, as his chute popped open.

Momo selected the toy because of what it represented. Our grandfather, Pop-Pop, had served in the air force in World War II. After sixty-five missions his plane was shot down. He survived thanks to a parachute, which Kicki forever preserved in a box in the attic. We knew this story before anything.

One blustery morning, my aunt Ellen followed Jay and me down to the beach. Her arms were nestled into a sweatshirt, which she wore inside out. She said it was more comfortable that way, inside out. I sometimes wore my sweatshirts like that, too.

Jay Bird and I ran along the beach, launching the plastic man into the air and watching as his diaphanous chute popped open like the wings of a monarch. We kept throwing him higher and higher, until a gust of wind came. The parachute swept through the sky, landing him in the sea. We waited for the waves to wash him back, but the surf kept dragging him out. We were losing him. Jay began to cry, which made me start to cry. The tide was strong and the parachute man kept flowing farther out to sea. In our small world it was a devastation. We looked back to Ellen. She understood.

Ellen unbuttoned her jeans and tossed off her inside-out sweatshirt. She dove into the freezing waves. We watched, fearful, as the churning surf swallowed her strokes. It took her a long time, but she reached the soldier, that damned trinket, floating like a loose bag beyond the sand bar. She stumbled ashore, teeth clattering, but she was smiling.

———————

We went to the side gate of the Memory Motel, where the owner gave us neon wristbands. I had sobered up from the beach, and the anxiety was creeping back. I needed to get drunk again.

As many times as we'd gone to the Mem that summer, none

of us had been inside the bedrooms except for Mike. They were exactly how we had imagined them: sparsely arranged with utilitarian furniture, everything covered with a layer of dust. A cheap acrylic chandelier dangled from the ceiling, striking the black floor with jagged light. There was a large mirror streaked with dead bugs and a low standing dresser made of unfinished wood. The walls were bare and hospital white. Twin beds had been removed and were stacked against the wall in the adjoining room. Under other circumstances the conditions would be frightening. We were thrilled to be there.

"This is the room the Clue board forgot," said Timmy.

I fixed myself a Ketel and Red Bull and helped Mike set up the music.

"Is everything okay, Drama?" he asked me. "You seem out of it."

I forced out a laugh, dismissed him with a headshake.

"Me? I'm totally fine. Just need this Red Bull to wake up. Cheers."

We had managed to shanghai an extra fifteen wristbands and kept running in and out to give them to our friends. Soon our party suite was packed. When I went to explore the adjoining room with Timmy and Colby, it seemed to be under renovation. The walls were stripped to wood beams, and the floors had been pulled up and layered with plywood. A toilet in the corner of the room was walled off on only two sides.

"Oh. My God." Timmy halted. Next to the stacked beds sat a massive Pink Panther head, the plush component of a knockoff costume. The kind people wore around Times Square. With great ceremony, Timmy and I lifted the massive mask onto Colby's head.

The night dervished into a disordered swirl. I went through the motions. I drank a lot. People peered into our roped-off room, watching us dancing on the tables and dresser. The Pink Panther head moved from person to person, a conch shell of mischief and debauchery. When Kirsten put it on, the weight of it toppled her over. At a certain point I got too drunk to feel anxious. I stopped thinking about Matt altogether.

D.Lo and Dana stepped outside for some fresh air. Dana was different from the other Hive girls. She had long brown hair and bangs and wore vintage clothes. A dress designer for a high-end fashion company, she spent most of her afternoons with a cup of coffee and a sketchpad, patrolling the universe for mystic inspiration.

"I'm never going to meet anyone," D.Lo lamented. "Every guy in New York is gay or a douchebag."

"D.Lo. Look at me." Dana grabbed her by the shoulders. "There are a bunch of sevens in our house, a few eights, a couple nines, but only one ten. You are the ten."

"I feel like a zero."

"That's your problem. You need to start acting like a ten."

"How?"

"Fake it."

"Fake what?"

"Fake like you're having the time of your life right now! No one wants to date someone who's sulking around. You need to exude confidence. You need to act like you're having *the best time ever*. It's how you pull positive people into your orbit. It's the law of attraction."

D.Lo was a wearing a black silk dress and the highest wedges she owned. She chugged the remainder of her vodka Red Bull.

"Let's go to the main bar."

Mike and Parker were in the adjoining room, their faces shadowed beneath the Mylar-backed light. They were talking about their mutual love of horror movies. They both loved to be scared.

At parties Mike normally flitted from person to person, extracting quips like nectar. He and Parker had been chatting for forty-five minutes. The energy between them was electric. When he looked into the other room and saw Shane wobbling across the black concrete floor, lips pursed, he felt trapped. Trapped, and guilty and confused.

Tyler walked into the adjoining room in the Pink Panther head. Mike pushed Parker in his direction.

"You should hook up with Tyler tonight," he whispered. "He's the best."

Parker turned to Tyler and his smile faded.

D.Lo and Dana ordered another round of tequila shots. The humid crush of bodies hemmed them to the bar.

"This is insane!" D.Lo said.

"I know!" Dana shouted back. "And it's not even midnight!"

The Mem's main bar glowed with beer signs and red lights. Strobes filled the air with frenzied energy.

"Wait, Dana. Is that a...bicycle?" D.Lo pointed to the bar's central pillar. A yellow bike wrapped around it just below the ceiling, its metal limbs like a pinwheel.

"Oh my God. Is that new?"

"How have we never noticed that?"

The bartender uncapped two Bud Lights. "Because you're always drunk," he said. "It's been there forever."

They orbited to the dance floor. D.Lo had started off faking it, but now she was having real fun. She let the strobes wash over

her, forgetting everything else. She was about to climb up onstage when a hand suddenly touched her arm.

"Hi," said a tall guy with blond hair.

"Hi."

His name was Everett. He was from Atlanta. They danced,
then went outside to talk. Somehow it came up that his mom
was a gynecologist. He had gone to Duke, worked for a start-up,
lived in the East Village, did a share in Hither Hills. They exchanged numbers.

"Do you want to come home with me?" he asked.

"Excuse me?"

"I said, do you... want to go on a date with me, this week,
or..."

"That's not what you said."

"I want to take you on a date," he repeated.

D.Lo was drunk, her energy fading. She had had her fill of
empty promises. She tossed her drink into the trash can.

"I'll believe it when I see it," she said, and went to hail a cab.

———————————

I woke up in the darkness of Bedroom 4 on the Navajo-print
futon. Tyler was cocooned on the air mattress. Next to him lay
Parker. I realized they must have hooked up.

Perrie was awake and searching for her keys. She wore a
macramé blanket over her shoulders. Despite the heat, she was
still cold. Mike was awake, too, and the three of us drove into
town for iced coffee. Along the way we passed Ashley, who was
already halfway into her five-mile run. Perrie beeped and waved.

"I don't know how she does it," she said. "Every morning.
Like clockwork."

"She's been coming to the SoulCycle studio, taking two, three classes a day," Mike said.

I watched her through the back window, running in her black sports bra, and my heart strained with a fierce and abiding loyalty. I saw in Ashley's obsessive exercising some of my own physical compulsions. I had been working out six, seven, sometimes eight times a week. The goal wasn't to get fit. The goal was to become unobjectionable.

"She's doing the bikini contest today," Perrie said. "Are you guys gonna go?"

Mike was smoking a cigarette out the window.

"Of course."

"She is legit crazy for doing this. I could never."

"You know what? Ashley may be crazy. But she's our crazy. I hope she wins the damn thing."

We went to the Sloppy Tuna that afternoon. The "fashion show" was held on the patio amid a cadre of day-drunk Manhattanites. We ordered our usual Transfusions and Rum Buckets from the bartender, who controlled the chaos with his soothing Australian accent.

The contestants were rated by round of applause. Ashley was the last to take the stage. The Hive took up the entire front row. We had pulled everyone we knew off the beach— our BC friends, our Montauk friends, our friends from other share houses.

The communal energy reminded me of my cousin Billy's basketball games, the way our family always occupied a huge swath of the gym. Some of my relatives, in the heat of the game, occasionally got ejected for their adversarial heckling. Others would grow pale and silent, almost too nervous to watch.

When Billy's team made the tournament, my aunt Ellen bought the younger cousins Hanes T-shirts and wrote CATHEDRAL BASKETBALL across them in purple Magic Marker. I was six years old, and I'd grow restless, sneaking away by myself to play under the bleachers. I climbed through the jungled beams, breathing in the scents—popcorn, sweat, floor wax, and the heavy perfume of the teenage girls who sat above. I'd find where my family sat, climb beneath them, and watch them watching the game.

When I came back, Kicki would give me a peppermint candy. I'd sit next to her while Billy drained threes. Everyone, myself included, screamed and taunted. But Kicki, who never missed a game, cheered with quiet pride. The point wasn't how loud you were. The point was that you were there.

"Our next contestant is Ashley from Alphabet City. Ashley loves football, tennis, and water sports. Please give a round of applause for Ashley."

Ashley slinked onstage in a lavender bikini laced with frills. She was by far the most striking contestant, but clearly the least comfortable. She was smiling sheepishly and pressing her palm to her face. It didn't matter. As she walked across the stage and waved, the crowd erupted. Everyone at the bar knew and adored her. Those who understood her felt a deep need to protect her. Ashley was the Mayor of Montauk. She was beloved. She had earned her free drinks.

After the beach we went to Cyril's, then Mike had an errand to run. I told him I'd go with him.

We were thinking about going to Ruschmeyer's that night but worried about the crowds. Of all the hot spots in Montauk, Ruschmeyer's had proven the hardest to penetrate. A chic, *Dirty Dancing*–style retreat, it echoed its own past as a summer camp—moonlit cabins, hammocks, a backyard strung with Chinese lanterns. At night people flooded the mess hall–style bar overlooking Fort Pond. A few times we'd managed to brave the line and ordered pitchers of the signature cocktail, the Ruschmeyer—a jalapeno-infused vodka drink mixed with muddled watermelon.

"We're going tonight," Mike said. "We have to."

Mike ran into 7-Eleven and I waited in the car. I was petrified to talk to him about Matt, but if I didn't soon I'd snap. He returned with a large hot coffee.

"This is the important errand you needed to run?" I asked. "A 7-Eleven coffee?"

"Trust me. You'll thank me in a minute."

The car ride was the perfect opportunity to talk to Mike. I summoned my courage.

"Can we have a real talk for a second?" I said.

"Of course. What's up?"

"It's stupid, and it's not a big deal. But I just need to talk through something."

"That's what I'm here for."

I'm falling in love with a guy. The words were right there, dangling in front of me, but as they were about to emerge they got washed away, lost in a cascade of conflicting thoughts. Was I gay? Could I never go back to dating girls? Did it matter? Would the rest of my friends care? Would I lose them? And then the big one: What would my family think? My parents were Massachusetts liberals, emotionally intuitive and culturally evolved. But they had few openly gay friends. They had built their lives around my future, and that future involved a wife. Would my happiness come only through the destruction of theirs?

I mentally flashed through every person in my family. My aunts, my uncles, my three waves of cousins. The entire gymnasium. As they appeared before me, my brain mined data I hadn't realized it had stored. My cousin Tony was good friends with a lesbian coworker, so maybe he'd be accepting. My cousin Mikey had dated a girl who turned out to be a lesbian, so maybe he wouldn't. My aunt Trisha was the least judgmental person I knew. My uncles were masculine, with a blue-collar aesthetic. I'd heard my cousins call people fags. But back then I had, too. And didn't my family love me unconditionally? Didn't we embrace each other no matter what? I had to believe that they'd accept me, if this ever turned into anything. The alternative was too painful to interrogate, and in that moment I was too locked into the microworld of my emotions to see anything with clarity.

"That Shark Attack party, is it even worth it? I don't think I want to go."

"Oh, that? I don't think I'm gonna go, either. You're totally fine."

We circled around Fort Pond, passing ranch houses with basketball hoops and truck beds with surfboards. My window was down, my leg leaning against the window. We pulled into Ruschmeyer's and drove up to the backyard entrance, tires pluming clouds of dirt.

"Dave!" Mike called to a man in a white golf shirt.

"Yo, Mike!"

The man was tan with a hardened face. I recognized him as the bouncer from one of the nights we braved the line. Those nights he had seemed impervious to emotion, but now, upon seeing Mike, his expression brightened.

"Large hot. Half-and-half, one Splenda," Mike said.

"I can't believe you remembered! Thank you! Will I see you later?"

"You bet."

Mike did things like this. He befriended the right people; he listened and remembered. His gestures were self-serving, obsequious, his motives comically transparent. But his actions stemmed from a genuine interest in others. Throughout the summer he delivered doughnuts to the Surf Lodge parking attendant. He met the owner of the Mem and attended an art show for his sister. He helped a Sloppy Tuna bartender launch her surf company's website. In Montauk you didn't need wads of cash to get VIP treatment. All it took was a friendly conversation, or a cup of coffee made the right way.

I'd squandered the perfect opportunity to talk through my feelings that afternoon, and as the day wore on I thought of little else. A prickling shame waxed over me. I'd have to weather my emotions on my own.

Back at the house the finance bros were getting ready for Shark Attack. Bradley donned a Hulk Hogan tank top, leopard-print pants, and lime-green Wayfarers. His girlfriend, Nadia, painted everyone's cheeks with tribal neon. To Bradley, a small-town Vermonter, Montauk was the crown jewel of a well-rounded city life. When he moved to New York he knew hardly anyone. Now, two years later, he had a thriving career and a healthy relationship. He had a summer house in Montauk. He had real friends, and he was happy. I envied his lightness.

In the Game Room I watched Bradley cut lines of coke with his Amex gold card. Arthur was still in his bathing suit and had no intention of changing.

"How many do you want?" Bradley asked me, his card clapping the wall mirror that had been laid across the pool table.

"I'm good, dude. Thanks, though."

"You sure, man?"

Tap. Tap. Tap. Tap. Tap. The sureness of this act. The ritual.

"Yeah, bro. I'm not even going to Shark Attack. Sounds wicked fun, though."

I watched the lines take shape, glowing like strands of silk. What did the finance bros think of me? Did they sense my internal reckoning? Did they lump me in with Colby and Mike? Or did they view me as one of them?

I had an instant connection with Colby, Timmy, and of course Matt. But I was also developing close bonds with the bros, Arthur especially. He was gregarious and easygoing, oblivious to cliques and divides. He was single, fit, and handsome. Girls liked him and he liked girls. But inside he still felt like the overweight nerd he'd been growing up. In high school he'd joined the swim team and his body changed. To psych himself up before his events, he'd imagined his opponents laughing at him. His insecurities could fuel him to victory.

"Who was that brunette girl you were talking to last night?" Arthur asked me. "In the VIP room?"

"Oh, that was Francesca. Just a college friend."

"Just a friend, sure," he joked.

Francesca and I had chatted for nearly an hour. Her grandmother had died and her mother was struggling. No doubt we'd transmitted an emotional intensity.

"Looked like more than friends to me," he said.

"Ha, well. You never know."

I sipped my beer. I was more or less sober. Arthur's country music was blasting from the boom box.

"Dude, we've got one more line," Bradley said to me. "You sure you don't want it?"

I looked around at the Day-Glo streaks and stars-and-stripes regalia. The last line was a smear, reflecting its own deviance. Without a Shark Attack ticket, I didn't really see the point in indulging, but part of me knew what that line represented. A bond. A proving ground. A way in. With a gutting desperation, I touched the bill to my nose and breathed in.

We went to Ruschmeyer's and took photos of the Chinese lanterns. They were orb-shaped and the color of cream. Some were big and some were small. Their proportions evoked a solar system within the trees, a distance and space I cosmically assimilated.

Nick Tot was inside on the dance floor, and Kirsten was avoiding him. Stefano texted her from the Mem, and she campaigned for us to go to town. We drained our watermelon drinks and texted for Henry's van. We always moved as a pack, rarely splitting up, even when it made little logistical sense. Once we'd found everyone in the crowds, we thanked Dave the bouncer and headed outside. We got in the van, all twenty of us, stacking the seats three deep. Mike was in the way back, knees buckled against the door. He texted Parker. We're on our way to the point. Fuck shark attack and come.

We bounced between the Point and the Mem until two in the morning. I won the favor of the corner bartender and she gave me a free Bud Light. Her name was Jade and her shoulders were covered in ornate mythic tattoos. Over a shared tequila shot she confessed she had a crush on Ashley. I told her she was in good company.

I waited in the bathroom line, the doors swinging open and shut. I spotted a man between the urinals sprinkling cocaine between his thumb and pointer finger. Someone attempted to cut the bathroom line, and the guy behind me called him out. The cutter spun back and head-butted him, shattering the man's nose in a gruesome spray of blood.

The Mem could be rough-and-tumble, but I'd never witnessed that kind of barroom violence up close. The chaos of the attack was destabilizing. Bouncers descended and the police arrived. D.Lo and I vacated to Pizza Village and split a cab home.

"He texted me this morning," she said in the cab. "The kid I was a bitch to at the Mem. I was convinced I'd blown it."

"That's great! Sounds like you didn't."

"He asked me on a date for when we're back in the city. First time I met someone at the Mem and actually got a text back."

"Made at the Mem," I joked. "Watch this guy turn out to be your husband."

"What the *fuck*!" D.Lo shouted as she walked into the Hive living room. I was holding our large cheese pizza a few steps behind her. As I reached the hallway I saw it, too. Shane was passed out on the staircase, bent at the waist like an abused Ken doll.

"Shane!" D.Lo yelled.

He was lying at such an unnatural angle that I momentarily worried he was dead.

"Shane, what the hell!" D.Lo pulled his arm and it dropped like a sandbag. His gingham shirt was unbuttoned. White jeans smeared with dirt.

"Shane, get up!" she yelled.

A low groan, a leg twitch. I attempted to turn him over. His eyes flickered as he slowly came back to life.

"Let me sleep," he mumbled.

"Dude, you're on the staircase!" I said. "At least sleep on the floor."

"No."

"For someone who's all about class, this is *not* classy, Shane!" D.Lo huffed.

"Fuck you," he slurred through pursed lips.

D.Lo tried pulling him up again, but he remained obstinate. "Fine," she said. "I'm leaving you on the stairs. You're a train wreck this summer, Shane. What the hell happened to you?"

She stepped around him and went straight to bed.

———————

As we gathered for Morning Therapy, Shane moved about the house as if nothing had happened. While the rest of us convalesced in gym clothes and pajamas, he was already in pressed chinos and a button-down. He took breakfast orders and I joined him for the ride into town.

"You were passed out on the staircase," I told him. "D.Lo and I tried to wake you, but you claimed you were comfortable. Do you remember?"

"Not at all." He laughed. "Was my head facing up the stairs or down?"

"Up, which I guess is better."

We drove past the hillside motels—the Briney Breezes, the Beachcomber, the Breakers. Power lines ebbing and flowing between telephone poles.

"Well at least I woke up in my bed. Parker was somehow on our floor this morning."

While we waited for our Bake Shoppe order we perused A Tale of Two Sisters, the bookshop next door. Shane liked nonfiction, especially histories and memoirs of political figures. He read the newspaper every single day, and it fueled his pessimism. He'd rather be islanded away from everything.

"This is the first Fourth of July that I'm not on Nantucket," Shane said as we got back into the car with egg sandwiches and iced coffees. "I've gone pretty much every year of my life."

"I've never been to Nantucket," I said.

"Oh, everything about it is *very* intentional. People use their houses to craft a narrative. Your Nantucket house is an extension of yourself."

"Yeah?" I was sipping my iced coffee, not really listening. I tended to zone out when Shane started talking about things like this.

"I had my first gay encounter out there," he said. "But I'm sure you don't want to hear about that."

"No, go ahead. Tell me."

"I met these two guys at a house party, they were friends of friends. They were beautiful. Tall, blond, tan, perfectly dressed. Rich. I was acting coy around them all night, but I was obsessed with them. I ended up going back to their home. We all hooked up in an outdoor shower. The water was like, dripping down their abs. It was the hottest thing."

"That's cool."

"I miss abs. God knows Mike doesn't have them. Anyway, I'm going to Nantucket for my friend Clarice's wedding at the end of July. Flying private. I need a break from this dumb Montauk scene."

I had a nickname for Shane when he got like this. I called him Shunt. A pretty self-explanatory portmanteau. I unwrapped my egg sandwich and started eating. I didn't want to engage.

———

As we were driving back, Mike woke slowly. His limbs ached. He was thirsty. A slant of light spilled across the orange carpet, illuminating Parker's curled-up body. Parker's eyes were slipping open, too.

"Why are you on the floor?" Mike rasped.

"I..." Parker smiled, embarrassed. He had used a folded beach towel as a pillow. "I don't really remember."

Mike made room on the bed and Parker climbed in.

"Tell me about Shark Attack," Mike said.

"It was insane. Like a rave, but in a country club. I'm glad I met you guys in town."

"I'm glad you did, too."

Parker turned over to face the door. They were silent for a few minutes, drifting in and out of sleep. Voices carried from the living room. A discussion about balloon curls. Something about a Princess Diana Beanie Baby, Adderall, and molly. A joke about Taylor being high on Plan B. Parker slid closer and they began to spoon.

Mike feigned sleep, but inside, his pulse blared. Parker's body was birdlike, breakable, the opposite of Shane's. He fit perfectly into the crook of Mike's arm. Mike felt himself growing hard. He arched away so Parker wouldn't realize. Parker took Mike's hand and rested it on his stomach, just above the line of his gym shorts.

Mike knew he should feel guilty, but the thrill of transgression was too intoxicating. It was a forbidden moment, amplified by their stillness. Parker leaned into Mike, and Mike's hand reached beneath Parker's elastic waistband. They lay like that until they heard the sliding door in the living room and Shane's voice, their infatuation solidified by what they hadn't done.

On the last night of the holiday weekend, we built a bonfire on the beach. Our BC friends brought beer, and other houses came. I imagined the tableau from the sea, all the bonfires lining the coast like a pagan bacchanal. We roasted marshmallows and danced in the cold sand.

Mike was drunk and emotional. I sensed something was wrong. Once again I considered telling him about Matt, but when he pulled me down to the coastline, I knew that he was not in a good place.

"What's wrong?" I asked.

He sipped his beer and looked over his shoulder. He took a moment to gather himself.

"I've been with Shane for five years," he said. "I love him."

"And you're worried about his drinking," I said.

"Yes. But it's not that. It's Parker. I have a crush on him. I...I don't know what to do."

I flashed back to the night Mike pulled me out to the student parking lot to tell me he was gay. That revelation, like this one, was monumental, but not surprising.

Now he was on the verge of tears, his hands shaking. I did my best to calm him down.

"We'll figure this out when we get back to the city," I promised. "Just try to relax and have fun tonight. It'll all be okay."

I realized, after, that I was invoking my mom. Her boundless ability to de-escalate and affirm. To encourage and guide. Her comforting assurances, like laundry warm from the dryer. I pictured those cloudy beach days when I'd dunk myself in the tide and then race back to her arms. She'd wrap me in a warm, dry towel and hold me, the towel becoming an extension of her. Swaddled, I'd sit on her lap in a beach chair and gaze out to sea. The water looked calm and safe.

I'd borrowed from her tool kit that night to support my friend, knowing in turn that I would soon call on him to support me.

Chapter Fifteen

By mid-July Montauk reached its zenith. Days were long and slow, nights tinted with the feel of summer camp. As June/July and July/August leases overlapped, the share house population doubled. I bumped into random friends from college, childhood neighbors, old acquaintances from high school. In Montauk everyone converged. I felt lucky to have all three months.

Every Friday inspired an uprush of freedom, a sense of possibility. People around us were falling in love. When Hicks, a second-year Hiver and NBC account manager, brought his boyfriend to Montauk, they whispered "I love you" for the first time, shrouded in the thick dark of the Hive's chambered basement. D.Lo and Everett went on that date in the city, then another at the Montauket, an old salt hotel with the best views of sunset. They'd spent every subsequent night together. We joked that, like in the Rihanna song, they'd fallen in love in a hopeless place—the dance floor of the Mem.

I had hoped my feelings for Matt might dissipate, but as the days pressed on they only grew stronger. I still hadn't told anyone, and the secret was rapidly consuming me. I envisioned the conversation I'd have with Mike, rehearsing it in my head. In my imagined version, the exchange always went well and I felt better. But I was too daunted to convert thought to action.

I spent the following weekend with my parents and the next in Boston for a wedding. I hadn't seen Matt in three weeks and the distance further galvanized my feelings. Alone, I was free to craft increasingly elaborate visions of my life. Imagined scenarios, unchecked fantasies, cosmic versions of my future self. I had spent so much time haunted by an unnamable malaise. Now my past loneliness felt directional. I somehow believed it was leading me to the kind of mystic love my family extolled.

Matt and I were both heading out east the next weekend. The Hive promised a quiet weekend with just six housemates on the schedule. I awaited Friday with anxious anticipation. At that point my travel routine was highly ritualized. I took the 1:45 train from Hunter's Point and spent the three-hour block immersed in writing, a bodega iced coffee next to me in a paper bag. When Matt and I had discussed our plans over Gchat, he'd asked if we could go out to Montauk together. He could leave work early to join me. It would be fun to ride out on the same train.

We arranged to meet at Bryant Park. As I walked down Avenue of the Americas, bag slung over my shoulder, I bucked the tides of a rising insecurity. Was he looking forward to seeing me? Was he confused about what I represented? Perhaps I had assigned too much importance to our night on the roof.

I stressed about the details of my clothes and the lay of my hair, stopping twice to check myself in my phone camera. My shoulders looked too narrow, and my eyes were rimmed with dark circles. As I reached the corner of Forty-Second, I braced myself for the inevitable thinning of whatever magic we'd conjured.

"There you are!" Matt called from down the street. He carried his sport coat and a leather bag. His polished shoes glinted. I'd never seen him in work clothes. The tailored wardrobe suited him. He looked staid but capricious, like someone pretending to be an adult.

We hopped on the 7 and took it two stops into Queens, sitting beneath rainbow ads for the famous dermatologist Dr. Zizmor. I found Matt's intense aquamarine eyes hard to meet and remember keeping my sunglasses on the whole ride. His Irish skin had grown tan, his nose freckled. His black hair had lightened to streaks of auburn.

"I hate it," he said, swiping his bangs. "I'm wearing a hat all weekend."

"No, it looks good. The sun must've been strong in P-town. Was it fun?"

"It was fine," he said, his face vacant.

"Just fine?"

"Yeah. I don't know. It was a lot."

"Drama?"

"No, not really drama. Just. I don't know. How's the Hive been? How was the Fourth?"

166

I sensed his evasion, but I didn't want to pry—not only for the sake of his privacy, but for fear of what I might find out.

"Oh, you know. Shane blacked out. D.Lo fell in love. Perrie got drunk and made out with a lawn chair. Standard weekend."

The subway reached Hunter's Point and we followed the stream of weekenders up the platform, climbing a set of grease-stained stairs into the sun. We bought our tickets for the LIRR and boarded the empty train, stretching our legs across a four-seater. Time passed quickly. We talked about everything from F. Scott Fitzgerald to Britney Spears. He told me about his childhood dog, a soft-coated wheaten terrier named Millie, and his first CD, *The Immaculate Collection* by Madonna ("It should've been a dead giveaway.") He had been accepted to Boston College, too, and almost went. I wondered if our paths would've crossed earlier, and what difference it would've made. As we approached Westhampton my anxiety dissolved. Our connection buzzed stronger than ever. At Montauk we took a cab to the Hive and it dropped us off at the foot of our street.

"Think we'll be the first ones here?" he asked.

"I bet. The house is basically empty this weekend. I hope it's still fun," I said.

"It will be. It could just be the two of us, and we'd still have a great weekend. As long as you're here, I'm good."

We walked up the steep damp road, the house in view.

"Same" was all I could manage to say.

We were inseparable that weekend, our internal clocks in sync. When one was hungry, the other hunted for food. When one started drinking, the other kept pace. We got up early, went for runs. We lay next to each other on the beach. We were beer pong partners, tide walkers, secret keepers, Kadima opponents. We watched episodes of *The OC* beneath a knitted blanket.

Ashley noticed. "You two are so handsome," she said. She was cutting cherry tomatoes and rolling them in sliced turkey, a makeshift dinner. "You are like, the best of friends."

Friends—was that what we were? I'd spent the past two months searching for certainty. Was our connection real? Was I making this up? I was so overwhelmed by my feelings that I no longer trusted my judgment. Ashley's validation calmed some of my nerves, but I knew I was hemmed in by my established sexuality. I wanted to be more than friends, but I didn't know how to broach it. And even if I managed to, how would he respond?

Matt and I pregamed hard Friday night. Shot after shot of Milagro tequila, cold Bud Lights on the moonlit deck. I went upstairs and kept Ashley company while she straightened her hair. She was more determined than usual to meet someone that night.

"It's almost August," she said. "I need to run into my Sloppy Tuna man again. I haven't seen him since that June day in the city."

She was sitting on a tufted seat fixing her eyelash extensions. The small table was a mess of products—powder palettes, brushes, bronzer, balm, lipstick. She ordered her foundation from France. It could mask the severest hickey with just a few dabs.

"You're gonna meet someone tonight," she said. "I feel it. Tell me your type. What are you looking for? I'll find her for you."

I was inches away from telling her everything. A few uttered words. Contortions of the tongue. I felt trapped behind glass.

"I don't really have a type," I said.

"I'm going to find you someone," she reiterated, clamping her hair for a second round of straightening.

I was a coward. I hated myself. I was lying by omission to everyone around me. I didn't have a type when it came to girls, but what was I looking for? The guy down in the kitchen. I should've told her. I shouldn't have wasted a moment.

I went back to the living room, where the others were waiting for a cab.

"Is Ashley almost done?" asked Kirsten.

I nodded, looking around. Matt was passed out, facedown on the couch.

"He's out for the count," Kirsten said. "Too much Tina Juice."

The van's headlights cut through the curtains. I ran back to the kitchen and grabbed the Milagro bottle, a couple inches still sloshing around. I drank until my eyes watered. Then I paused and drank the rest.

Just as we pulled up to the Point, the tequila hit. I stepped out of the cab and regained my balance. Too much brown liquor made me morose and withdrawn, but tequila seemed to do the opposite. I was bombed but energized. I could feel the vibrations of the night.

The Point was crowded, as usual. Tori, a beloved Montauk resident, was working the door. On busy nights she charged us the fifteen-dollar cover, but she'd often let us cut the line. I handed her my money and held my wrist out for the stamp.

"Thanks, Tori," I said, kissing her on the cheek as I walked in. I was getting to know people. I was remembering.

Our BC girlfriends (my Tribeca neighbors) were already inside drinking Tito's and soda with lemon. We found them in the far corner decked in wedges and loose sleeveless tops.

"I texted you!" Mike yelled to Caroline above the music.

"Please." She shoved him. "This is Montauk. You know we don't carry our phones."

They'd lost so many valuables to the "Montauk Monster" that summer that they started traveling light. Wallets, too, were dispensed with. Caroline was leaning against the counter for another drink, a golden flash tattoo gilding her arm.

"Charlotte," she snapped. "Hand me the Mutual Fund."

Charlotte produced a clear Ziploc. It contained a credit card, a single ID, and loose crumples of salt-watered cash.

"What the hell is that?" Mike balked.

"It's our purse," she replied, relishing Mike's shock. He grabbed the bag on its way to her. Its contents slid into his palm.

"Ricardo Sanchez? This isn't even a female ID!"

"Charlotte just used it at the Mem."

"This debit card says Preferred Customer."

"My replacement's in the mail."

When the bartender saw their Ziploc, he gave her the vodka soda for free.

We danced to a medley of Motown songs until the body heat grew too stifling. Mike tapped his cigarettes. He was looking to the cordoned-off outdoor space in the parking lot.

When I offered to join Mike outside I had all but given up on the idea of confiding in him about Matt. I'd spent the past few weeks lost in my wayward thoughts, and realized I needed time to process things on my own.

I decided I'd let the summer run its course first. Once I had a better grip on my emotions, I'd consider opening up about them. When and if the time came, I'd tell Mike in a private setting, undiluted by rivers of tequila.

This is what I told myself. This is not what happened.

That night, drunk at the Point, I told Mike everything.

Chapter Sixteen

Mike became my confidant, my coach, my aider and abettor. His reaction had been instant and unequivocal—he completely supported me and acknowledged my internal struggle. He was honored I had confided in him and he vowed to be discreet. I told him I was less concerned about others knowing than I was about dealing with my crush.

"Regardless," he'd said. "It's your news to share."

I filled the role of ingénue, peppering him with questions. Mike understood that we were different. I had a baseline attraction to girls that complicated my position. I struggled with how to square these divergent urges. I had learned about the Kinsey scale in college. I'd grown up watching Mischa Barton experiment with Olivia Wilde on *The OC* and knew multiple bisexual women. But Mike and I both acknowledged the difficulties that spectrum-surfing men faced within our peer group. This was before sexual fluidity was normalized. To my mind, a guy who sucked a dick would always be perceived as gay. I feared that by openly admitting my feelings for Matt, I'd destroy any chance of ever again being with a woman. But I was so in love with him that I didn't care. I'd risk the chance of being alone forever.

"Can I tell you something?" Mike asked as we walked along the beach the next weekend. "I never felt a connection with another guy until college. It took meeting a specific guy to make it real."

"Really?" I thought back to our senior year, the way Mike returned to campus with his drastic new look. It was as though he'd pressed a button and "become" gay.

"Who was it?" I asked.

"It was Evan."

Evan, our college roommate. My current roommate in Tribeca. He was up in Rochester that weekend with his girlfriend Lizzie.

"Wait, you and Evan...But...?"

"Ha, no, Evan is straight. But I told him how I felt about him one night. He was great about it. It brought us closer together as friends. Plus it opened me up to the possibility of meeting someone new. For you it's different, of course. But Matt is a good guy. He has a good heart. And I've been watching you two interact, it's definitely mutual."

"You...you think?"

"One *hundred* percent."

I was less sure. On the beach Sunday afternoon Matt seemed distracted and withdrawn. He was glued to his phone. I'd lain on my stomach, sun blading my back, listening to the vibrational volley of his text exchanges. Twice he left to make phone calls.

"Everything's fine," he assured me when he got back. "Stuff at work."

We went to Swallow East, a restaurant on the docks. On Sundays a reggae band played songs on a steel drum. Everyone went barefoot, kicking their sandals into a pile by the stage. We listened to "High Tide or Low Tide" as the sun dipped behind the fishing boats. Mike ordered us small plates—crispy fish tacos, orzo mac and cheese, asparagus fries, wedge salad, brisket. The calamari was sweet and spicy, glazed in a duck sauce and sprinkled with peanuts. Everything looked delicious, but I could barely eat. Matt's withdrawal had left me disoriented. I retreated inward, into my insecurities, into the darkness that skulled me.

Ashley, too, seemed to exist in a constant state of heartache. Her recent love interests had not panned out. With every new guy, she fell fast and hard. She did little to protect her heart, which was what drew so many to her. I admired her tendency to love deeply, but I hated to see her suffer. That summer we occupied the same vulnerable hutch.

Every morning Ashley went to breakfast at an Italian restaurant in Midtown Manhattan. She ordered a wheat croissant with raspberry filling and a skim cappuccino. The bathroom attendant was a wrinkled woman who didn't understand English very well, but Ashley liked to talk to her anyway. In college she had played varsity tennis. The admissions office approached her during her junior year and took her picture sitting on the court. She wore sunglasses, a high ponytail, and the red Dragon Adidas sneakers she reserved for match play. She was the only one on the team who had walked on. After the photograph, they asked her a few questions about how Providence College made her a better person. She was no longer the mean girl she'd been in high school. She assumed the brief profile would run in a collage at the back of the brochure. When the catalog arrived, she opened it to a two-page spread with the headline BECOMING ASHLEY.

Ashley and I stayed out that Sunday and drove back to the city before dawn. Route 27 felt smooth and quiet, tinged with a lonesome pale light. In the back of her car lay some wedge shoes and running gear. CFA books were piled in the space behind the headrest. Despite the early hour we were both chatty and alert. She told me about a failed relationship with a coworker who had once been her best friend. He had left her gutted. It was over, but they still talked.

"I wish I were more like Kirsten," she said. "She can see the beauty in heartbreak. But I can't. I just feel like I can't breathe."

I paused as she described her anguish, aware that she was tracing the contours of my own tortured heart.

Chapter Seventeen

The city was in the midst of a heat wave. In Tribeca we ate ice cream as the AC hummed, the lights browning and dimming, then flickering back. The subway platforms baked to a boil.

Wednesday was Tyler's birthday. The Hive planned to celebrate at Beekman Beer Garden. I left work and walked to Forty-Second Street to catch the 2/3 train to Fulton. Times Square was a hot blur of movie billboards and soda ads, transfixed playgoers and incandescent lights. I listened to my iPod and tried to contain my nervous energy. I'd been on edge since the weekend, plagued by a pervasive sense of ineptitude. My crush on Matt held me captive.

I walked through the Financial District to the East River. The Beekman occupied a wharf adorned with plush white chairs, beach umbrellas, and imported sand. I bought a Belgian ale crushed with an orange slice and found my housemates barefoot on the artificial beach.

"This is like, the earliest I have ever gotten out of work, ever,"

Timmy said. He wore tight-fitting dress pants and a starched shirt, a work persona at odds with the weekend Timmy I knew. "I can't believe Tyler isn't even here yet. Who else is coming?"

"Shane'll be here in a minute," said D.Lo, looking down at her phone. "Matt's on his way."

"Wait," Timmy said, flinging his arm at D.Lo. "Let's *talk* about Matt."

"What about?"

I was standing barefoot in the sand, looking out to the Brooklyn Bridge, listening but not listening. My body must've anticipated it because I could feel the blood draining from my face, my chest knotting, my heartbeat quickening. In the glaring heat my skin went cold. Timmy tilted his head, eyes confiding.

"I hear Matt has a new man."

I took a sip of my beer, tasting the sweet cut of the orange, my dread mounting. D.Lo confirmed Timmy's statement, her words dismantling the beams of my elaborate inner world.

They'd met in P-town. They'd hit it off instantly. They'd spent almost every night together since.

I stayed for another drink, my awkwardness palpable. Matt came and I forced myself to act normal. No one made any mention of his new man, and neither did he. I wore a smile the entire time, sadness rotting me from the inside out.

―――――――

"Okay, here's the thing," Mike said the next night. We were sitting on the wobbly bar stools of Pete's Tavern, drinking tequila, our voices muffled by the copper ceilings. "Matt's guy is twice his age. He's a novelty. It's not serious and it won't last."

Gossip hotwired through the Hive, traveling down reliable pathways. I had learned all the details about Matt's new love interest, the cookie crumbs on social media revealing themselves in hindsight. It shocked me that Matt could spark with someone so much older. I had grown convinced that we shared a heart, but his new connection fell outside the scope of my impulses. Was he truly attracted to this person? Did he gravitate to him emotionally? I was mourning the loss of a relationship I'd never had. I nodded along to Mike's encouragement, but the heartsickness was overpowering.

"You two would be perfect together," Mike said. "Just let this play out."

Mike himself was in no better shape. Since the Fourth of July his crush on Parker had grown like ivy. They were meeting at dive bars during the week, getting wine drunk, talking for hours, texting the whole next day. Mike got home from these meet-ups at one or two, then woke up at four for his opening shift at Soul-Cycle.

You know he likes you, right? Shane had said one night, smelling the liquor on Mike's breath. *He likes you, and you're gonna break his pathetic little heart.*

Mike had shrugged Shane off, but knew he had a point. Their desires were apparent. But Shane had one thing wrong. Mike wasn't going to break Parker's heart. Parker was already breaking his.

I needed a breath, a moment to recalibrate. I had passed through the week in a dense fog of sadness. It took every ounce of energy

I had to maintain a façade of workplace cheer. My feelings for Matt felt like a missed opportunity. The universe had given me one shot, and I'd been too afraid to take it. I went out to Montauk that weekend, relieved that Matt was not on the schedule.

On the beach that Saturday, I watched a guy playing Spikeball in a cranberry bathing suit. The Hive girls were slathering themselves in a mixture of Australian Gold tanning oil and coconut body lotion, and the scent bristled my nose. Perrie always applied self-tanner the night before, and so did Shane, but secretly. Sun In, too, was a clandestine indulgence. I returned my gaze to Cranberry Bathing Suit. He was shirtless, his face banded with sunglasses. He had the sharp jaw and etched abs of a Roman statue. I'd never seen anyone with such a perfectly proportioned body. Since connecting with Matt, I'd let more in. Privately I acknowledged that Cranberry Bathing Suit was hot. I stole glances over pages of *The Secret History*.

On the other side of us, our friends the Stavolas were playing volleyball. They were the ones we'd inventively nicknamed Volleyball Girl and Volleyball Girl's Sister before learning their real names. They'd grown up in Montauk and bemoaned its recent evolution. Once "a drinking town with a fishing problem," Montauk was becoming—somehow—hipster chic. Many worried it had lost its humble spirit. Signs were appearing throughout town: a fedora slashed with a red line above the words SAVE MONTAUK. I knew, as weekenders, that we were part of this unwelcome influx.

"Mm-hmm." Colby nodded to Kirsten from his beach chair. "Girl, check out that eye candy. He is fine."

Cranberry Bathing Suit was leaning over with his hands on his thighs. His abs were flexed.

"Oh my God," said Kirsten. "I've been eye-fucking him all afternoon."

"The cranberry bathing suit?" said Perrie. "Me too!"

"Holy shit, me also!" said Tyler.

"Ugh, he's mine!" said Kara.

Cranberry dove for the ball, his sweat mixing with the sand. The Hive ogled. Even the finance bros offered their admiration. I wanted to chime in and knew I could have without controversy; people would've taken it in jest. I considered it, but remained silent. I was too uncomfortable to join the chorus, and the moment passed.

That night at the Mem, I wingmanned for Arthur. He was trying to hook up with a girl from the Meeting House, a share near the pond. I flirted with her friend, bought her a drink, trying to will myself to be into it. With Matt not around, it seemed like a good opportunity to revisit the world of heterosexuality. But the whole thing felt hollow. It carved me empty. When Arthur failed to connect we went back early, the air still heavy with humidity.

"Let's go in the pool!" Colby suggested as we got back to the house. We were still sweating from the Mem and not in the mood for sleep, so we changed into our bathing suits and ventured down the cascading wooden staircase, our footsteps swallowed by the dark. The pool sat at the bottom of the backyard, fifty yards down. It was outfitted with a starched-white diving board, a basketball hoop, and a sun-faded slide. We felt the water with our toes. It glowed a shocking neon blue.

We played a few rounds of Marco Polo, drunkenly flailing and swallowing water. Arthur was it and counted to ten. I swam to the deep end and held on to the side. Colby swam up next to me.

I felt a hand slip under my bathing suit. Fingers searching for, and grabbing, my dick. I lurched away.

"Oh, come on," Colby said, swimming closer. His voice was crackly, his eyes distant. I could tell he was on the cusp of blacking out.

Marco.

"Colby, no."

He reached into my suit again and I was less resistant.

"Just let me play with it," he said. "It doesn't mean you're gay."

I treaded away, slowly, laughing a little, embarrassed by my arousal. "Colby."

He held my gaze. His eyes were piercing, blue and bloodshot with chlorine. He looked tired, hollow.

"Just, come on. I know you want it. No one has to know."

I wanted to run and hide. Colby's behavior that summer had grown increasingly distressing. He was picking fights with everyone and constantly stirring up drama, especially with the girls. I knew I needed to swim away and ultimately fended him off. But part of me wanted to carry him to a bedroom and lock the door.

Perrie woke up the next morning and got in her car. She rolled down the windows and turned up the music. In her glove compartment lay a notebook and a pen. She had a dock she liked to drive to.

She parked her car and strolled to the dock. In her notebook were the seeds of a long-germinating novel. She sat on the bench and began to write, a morning fog rolling across the sea. The best times at the Hive, she thought, were the times when you could slip away.

Chapter Eighteen

That Tuesday I received an email from my dad. It was a follow-up to a phone call we'd had on Sunday. Overwhelmed by the weekend, I had hinted at waves of heartache but offered no details beyond the backdrop, Montauk. My father assumed the object of my anguish was a girl.

Not sure what to say here..

Few thoughts..

* Weekend partyhouse may not be much of a place to look for a substantive romance to begin..host of reasons...

* Looking for something to happen may sometimes create unrealistic expectations or translate an undercurrent of urgency

* Weekend of drinking absolutely sets up tension, sense of vulnerability and depression

Now I'm sure what to say..

* Know who you are ... a great kid with strong core values

* Have strong faith that sticking to those core values will ultimately make the difference and define the success of your life

* You are deeply loved with good reason

SHBAL D

My dad's emails were akin to haikus. Sharp staccato sentences dredged with ellipses and the frequent asterisk. He signed them SHBAL, Study Hard Be a Leader, the sendoff we'd used since I was in first grade. A corollary to the "clear eyes, full hearts, can't lose" chant from *Friday Night Lights.*

My dad and I were both driven, soft-hearted, and prone to guilt. He was an involved and present father, and I loved him fiercely. He began sharing his wisdom with me from an early age. On car rides he'd quiz me on musical artists. *Who sings this one?* he'd ask, cranking up the oldies station. *The Four Tops. The Lovin' Spoonful. The Rolling Stones.*

He coached me in basketball and taught me to ski. We played Horse in the driveway and went for runs through the park. Then we'd order lunch at the Burger King drive-through and get an extra order of fries—road fries—which we'd share on the ride home.

I was an intermittently competitive but very anxious athlete. Nothing made my dad prouder than when I excelled in sports. In third grade, I made it to the state finals in the four-hundred-meter dash. The event was held in Braintree, Massachusetts, on the hottest day in July. I was issued a black T-shirt to run in. Around sundown I toed the start line as the official raised the gun. My dad held the camcorder. My mom cheered. A crowd ringed the track and filled the bleachers.

I had carried around the psychic pressure of the event for weeks, and then, as the gun went off, I merged my body with it. I hugged the first curve and sprinted down the straightaway, hugged the second curve, then eyed the finish. The setting sun was big and orange and caromed off the bleachers. I knew I wasn't going to win the heat, but the boy next to me was within my stride. I had to beat him. I had to. It meant everything, beating him. And when I did, my parents rushed the field and hugged me and handed me a red Gatorade. That was what I remembered most, the sweet Gatorade staining my mouth, and my dad—proud, happy, and approving.

———————

In mid-August D.Lo's grandfather died. After the funeral she went to the Hive with her sister. She needed a few days to decompress. Matt arrived that Friday with a box of treats from Insomnia Cookies, her favorite bakery. She had been inundated with thoughtful affirmations, but the most poignant condolences came from the Hive.

"I got more texts from the Hive than I did from my high school friends and college friends combined," she told Matt as she bit into a chocolate chip.

Life in the share house could be melodramatic. It could be hidebound and all-consuming. But our friendships were jeweled with a fierce loyalty. In times of need the Hive took care of its own.

I reached Montauk that weekend in a state of apprehension. I hadn't seen Matt since the Beekman and didn't know how I'd behave around him. My loneliness felt like a dark halo, visible to everyone. I searched out D.Lo and gave her a hug. She offered me a cookie. I found Matt's thoughtfulness deeply touching. He was first and foremost a good friend. I bit into a chocolate cookie, vowing to keep my emotions in check.

———

"The three of us are going to Surf Lodge," Ashley instructed. "If we go early, I can get us in." Matt and I were lying on Ashley's bed, staring at the ceiling. It seemed we had no choice in the matter. D.Lo and her sister had gone to dinner at Harvest, and the others had yet to arrive. I showered and dressed in my nicest outfit, J Brand jeans and a white linen button-down. Ashley's pearlized bag contained Life Savers mints, mascara, flash tattoos, one latex condom, a cell phone charger, and her hair straightener. Henry arrived in his MONTAUK'S BEST TAXI van.

"The bees are gonna get some honey taaannighhttt," he joked, the veins of his muscles bulging beneath his tank top.

The Surf Lodge was Montauk's buzziest hot spot, a dreamlike bohemia infused with meticulously curated art and sound. A former dive bar on the edge of Fort Pond, the twenty-room motel and restaurant hosted free concerts at sunset. A few years later an iconic artist would paint the lodge's white façade with a Day-Glo swirl, but that summer its lines were sharp and clean. The "Slodge," as we called it, was undoubtedly hip, but it channeled a polished, upscale vibe at odds with the community's shabby charm. When we went, we went begrudgingly, knowing we were part of a contentious scene.

Despite his new romantic interest, Matt and I struck the same natural rapport. He didn't mention his dating life and I didn't ask. The Surf Lodge was thronging with waiflike scenesters, travelers, and artists. We roamed the deck freely, taking in the lakeside views, the strings of lights, the glowing fire pits and pulsing tropical house music.

The night was sequined with fashion and glamour—exotic necklaces, man buns, pops of leather. At the outdoor bar we ordered Endless Summers—a vodka drink mixed with crushed grapes. We danced to eighties music in the vaulted barn, beneath the old surfboards that lined the rafters. Back outside, bathed in moonlight, Ashley stopped midstride.

"Oh my God." Her voice was barely above a whisper. "Guys. There he is."

Across the deck stood Ashley's Sloppy Tuna man. He was dressed simply, in a T-shirt, black jeans, and white sneakers. His teeth glowed white against his summer tan. I watched Ashley's shoulders straighten, her gaze intensify. She nervously flipped her hair.

"He's coming this way. I need to go up to him. I need to say something."

She knifed through the crowd, lashing her bag behind her.

Matt and I followed within earshot. We watched as she clasped his arm.

"Hi, do you remember me?"

"Uhhh...no."

"I saw you at the Sloppy Tuna over Memorial Day."

"What?"

"And we crossed paths one day outside the Madison Avenue Equinox."

"Oh...umm..." He was rubbing the back of his head, his hockey hair rustling. "I'm sorry."

"Well, I'm Ashley. It's nice to meet you."

"Nice to meet you, too?"

She turned to walk away. Even to an outside observer the exchange had been painful. I envied her courage but felt pangs of secondhand awkwardness.

"Hey, wait," he called, flummoxed. "Can I at least get your number?"

She turned back, tamping down a smile.

All roads led to Montauk, both figuratively and literally. That night at Surf Lodge the stars seemed closer, a promise of fates we might reach up and arrange. Stripped of the blaring obstructions of the city, Ashley sharpened her prayers. Montauk was a town built for kismet. A place where desire and destiny could overlap.

She got home that night and her phone buzzed. A lengthy text message scrolled down her screen, filling her with an unfamiliar joy. Sloppy Tuna Man was leaving for Yacht Week in Croatia. Would she like to get dinner when he returned? Yes, she thought. She would like that very much.

After Surf Lodge, Matt and I sat stargazing on the roof. We passed the aux cord back and forth, playing random songs from our devices. The others were inside.

I hit shuffle and "Mack the Knife" came on. The song reminded me of Kicki. I told Matt how I said little prayers to her on my morning walk to the subway.

"You must've been close with her," he said.

"She was my favorite person."

I tried to explain what Kicki had meant to me. I started with the small things. The way she always hung her laundry on the line. The way her beautiful penmanship resembled a crane opening its wings. She could have been an artist, an athlete. In one home video, she's in her Easter sweater, all five-foot-one of her, shooting free throws in my cousins' driveway. She swishes five in row.

On half days in the winter, she'd don a toggled coat and pick me up from school. Her car was a Crown Victoria the size of a small boat. The seat belts were encased with sheepskin pads. Over lunch she'd teach me how to draw. She'd play Crazy Eights with me. She took care of me when I was sick. She could peel an entire apple in one long waxy ribbon without it breaking.

"She seems like the best grandmother," Matt said. "I say little prayers to people, too."

We talked about how we prayed more to people than to God. We both sought religion through our relationships. Matt's best friend, Kelley, was coming to the Hive the last weekend, and he was excited to introduce her to all of us. They'd met their freshman year at college. She was one of the first people he came out to. They both loved Céline Dion. During their senior year, Kelley was taking a shower and felt a lump. She was twenty-two. She went for a mammogram and brought Matt with her. She was diagnosed with stage 3 breast cancer and underwent chemotherapy and radiation. The cancer was still there but under control.

"She spent a year working in DC and commuting home to Boston on the weekends for chemo. No one knew she was sick. She never once complained. She refuses to let it affect the way she lives her life. But it's the worst thing in *my* life."

I could see the pain in Matt's eyes. He was grappling with a fate he would never understand. I put myself in Kelley's position, imagining what my life would look like if I knew my time was short. The threat of looming regrets, of unsaid words. My heart hurt for Matt's friend, and for Matt.

"She sounds amazing," I said. "I can't wait to meet her."

"She'll love you, John." We were lying on our backs, our legs touching. "I can't wait for her to get to know you."

We stayed on the roof for hours, talking about everything from our families, to the books we wanted to read, to Hanson's attempted comeback. He told me about his crippling fear of death, and I described my pervasive loneliness. He wrapped his hand around my wrist. We were strong and broken in the same way.

Sunday arrived with its attendant torment. Some people wanted to stay out all day and go to dinner on Shelter Island. Others were scrambling back to the city. All of us suffered from a condition called the Sunday Scaries. The Scaries were a pathology of doom—born of alcohol consumption, impending work pressures, and existential dread. They struck without warning, descending like a dark curtain and lingering into Monday or Tuesday. Methods of treatment varied. Those lucky enough to have a partner clung tight. The less fortunate holed up with Netflix and Seamless. Others drank through them, or self-medicated in other ways.

"Mike, I need the Trail Mix!" Kirsten called from her cocoon. It was noon and she had yet to leave bed. Mike came in with his plastic bag of pills, placing a Xanax on her tongue.

We splurged on brunch at Navy Beach, a posh new spot on the Sound. Matt was on his phone most of the time, texting. He left for twenty minutes to take a call. This time I knew who was on the other end.

"Mike, I can't take it anymore," I broke down back at the house. "He's been texting and talking with his other guy all day. It's real."

We were alone in the kitchen, the others down by the pool. It was four thirty and Matt had just left for Manhattan.

"Look at it from his position. On paper you're still straight. You're not out. No one wants to be an experiment."

"It's not like that."

"No, I know. But he'd be right to have his guard up."

I felt myself starting to cry.

"I've been waiting so long to connect with someone, and now that I finally feel something it's making me feel even more alone."

"John, you're not alone. Every single person in this house loves you. I love you. You have so many amazing people in your life."

"I need to tell him."

"I agree. But you have to do it the right way. You don't want to scare him off. You need to . . . be more like Ashley."

I knew exactly what he meant. Ashley had mastered the strategic long game. Sloppy Tuna Man was proof of her mystic skill.

"Maybe I should talk to her," I said.

"You definitely should. She's great at this kind of stuff. Plus she knows Matt better than I do."

The Hive had thinned out; the basement lay empty. I moved my belongings upstairs, laying out a dress shirt and work khakis for morning. We were driving back at dawn and I planned to head straight to the office.

I reinflated an air mattress in the master bedroom where Mike and Kirsten were staying and unzipped a sleeping bag. I didn't want to sleep alone.

———

Ashley texted me that Monday at 11:38 a.m.

Hi love! I'm taking colby out for bday drinks tmrw night (prob at diablo) around 8—if you want to come surprise/join in, lmk! Xoxoxo

I'd reached a breaking point. I texted Ashley back.

Hey sounds good I'm in. And also—do you think there's any way just the two of us could grab a drink or a coffee or something this week? I'm in a bad headspace and need advice on something and I trust your opinion.

She wrote back immediately. Of course! What are you up to tonight? I get out of an eyelash appt at 6:20. Free from 6:30 on.

We met at Empellon Taqueria, a Mexican restaurant in the West Village. Ashley began most of her nights there. It was upscale and quiet, with white brick walls, gypsy lanterns, and floors of distressed wood. From there she could migrate to one of three preppy haunts: Village Tavern, Galway Hooker, or the Windsor.

We sat at the bar and ordered spicy margaritas, a large Dalí-esque mural reflecting my own mystification. In the glow of tequila bottles, words seemed to fail me. I didn't know if I was gay, straight, or bi, and I didn't know if that mattered. But I knew the straight persona I had inhabited all summer couldn't encapsulate my whole self.

"So what's up?" Ashley asked.

I took a deep breath and launched in, my voice quick and low. I told her everything.

She nodded, her face impassive. She spoke Matt's last name, like a question, as if to clarify.

"Yes. That Matt."

"Okay," she said. "Is he the first guy you've had these feelings for?"

"Yes. But I know this feeling. I've felt different versions of it before for girls. This is something even more intense."

She looked upset. I could tell she was fighting to maintain her composure. When she spoke again her voice was measured. "He's the best. I adore him."

"I'm sorry to fling this on you. I know it's probably unexpected."

"No, no. It's not that at all. This is the best thing I've ever heard. You and Matt mesh so perfectly. You have the same heart. You're so ideal for one another it makes me want to cry. It just..."

She hunted through her Mary Poppins bag for her phone and scrolled through her messages. "Look."

It was a text from Matt.

We met up last night and he asked me to be his boyfriend!! I said yes!! I can't believe this! I'm so happy!

I felt ill.

"When did he send this to you?"

"An hour ago."

I ordered another margarita, a shot of tequila, and a Tecate. I had never felt so devastated. Ashley did her best to lift my spirits. She wanted me to shift my thinking. Matt's new relationship would last two, three months tops, she said. This wasn't the end of our story. If I wanted to be with him, I'd have to be patient.

"You'll have to be strong. And strategic. But trust me. It's going to work out. I'm going to help."

Chapter Nineteen

Hello Bees!

If you're on this email, that means you're going out to the Hive for this coming weekend (8/23–8/25).

Some items *(READ THEY HAVE CHANGED)*

1) ABSOLUTELY NO MUSIC OUTSIDE. Keep every door closed and AC on. If we piss off the neighbor this weekend we are in trouble. If you see a neighbor, be nothing but kind and respectful.

2) Hive cups—we are down to 20. We started with almost 200. They are not allowed to leave the house and if you have any please return them.

3) Beds—Guests do not get beds, end of story. Beds

include airbeds as well. As for hive members, be respectful of each other. I can only police so much.

4) TV—I need two or three of our stronger hivers to help move the TV from the game room upstairs to the living room. If you could help me do this at some point you're exempt from cleaning.

5) It's Perrie's birthday on Saturday! We'll be having a pregame at the house followed by an early departure to Crow's Nest or Moby Dick's. (Unless she's too cold of course.)

6) Also, Congrats to Bradley on his engagement! Him and Nadia are both coming to the house this weekend so we have even more to celebrate. It's going to be a great weekend!

Room assignments below.

Our penultimate weekend shimmered with light. Matt was home for a wedding, clearing space for me to mentally restore. Bradley, one of my favorites of the finance bros, and his girlfriend, Nadia, were engaged, and the Game Room took on a festive air. People started arriving on Thursday night, splurging on rental cars or borrowing from the 'burbs. Everyone was going to call in sick on Monday. We never wanted to leave.

The house made room for twenty-six people, an all-star cast. Mike, Shane, Parker, D.Lo, Perrie, Kirsten, Ashley, Timmy, Tyler, and Arthur were all there, toasting to Bradley and Nadia. We were nearing the end, but refused to think about it. We were sun children chasing an eternal summer. Fall was a four-letter word.

On Friday we went to Lynn's Hula Hut, an open-air tiki bar pitched in the marina. Torches illuminated the hammocks, Adirondack chairs, and games of bag toss. Lynn herself was manning the bar. She was a salty spitfire with wild blond hair. Her cucumber-infused vodka drinks lulled me into a state of serenity. Calypso music morphed the air. It was a moment of relative peace. We grasped it, knowing it would not last.

As a kid, I watched the soap opera *All My Children*. The women in our family, including Kicki, were devoted fans, and in the summers my cousins and I tuned in with equal fervor. After swim lessons my mom would make lunch and we'd laugh at the outlandish plot twists and arch dialogue, the histrionic flare of Erica Kane. It was a soap opera in the grand tradition. Tornadoes, earthquakes, bombs, car accidents, heart transplants, pregnancies, miscarriages, weddings, and abductions all struck Pine Valley at the exact same time. If you fell off a waterfall and they found your body, you were dead. If you fell off a waterfall and they didn't find your body, you'd return four years later with amnesia. Everyone had an evil twin. Everyone got stuck in an elevator. Everyone hung out at the hospital. Everyone visited without calling. Everyone had just the right comeback. Everyone knew everyone.

All My Children had been canceled in 2011, but an online revival had launched that summer. I watched each night before sleep, comforted by the familiar characters and their improbable schemes. Pine Valley reminded me of my family. My mom and I texted about the story lines.

The Hive, I realized, was a real-life soap opera. Affairs, secrets, sickness and addiction, toxic love and boiling resentments—all found a place between the house's hot walls.

After the Hula Hut we rode into town. The Point wasn't too crowded, so we took to the dance floor. Mike and Parker were inseparable. They kept going shot for shot, their elbows touching.

On the way home, Shane was drunk and angry. He was convinced the cabdriver was trying to upcharge us. A smuggled drink sloshed in his hand.

The cab pulled into our driveway.

"I'm not paying for this," Shane huffed. We each owed ten dollars.

"Shane, come on," I said.

"Nope." He got out of the car and slammed the door. I hurriedly handed the driver a wad of cash, enough to cover us both.

"You owe me," I said to Shane as he sloped up the stairs.

"I don't owe you shit." He finished his drink and tossed the glass down the deck. "You can clean that up, too. God knows I've done enough for you and this goddamn house."

I'd spent all summer tolerating Shane's catty entitlement. I lost it.

"You haven't done anything for me," I yelled. "You've been a nonstop dick all summer."

"Fuck you, John."

"Fuck you, Shane. You're the fucking worst."

"No, *you're* the worst. You're worse than the worst. You're nothing. At least I know who the fuck I am."

I grabbed the wet glass, anger tapering through my veins. Had

I stopped to reflect, I would've realized why Shane was truly upset. He'd watched Mike and Parker dancing together all night. Their connection was obvious to everyone. Mike was pushing Shane out. But I couldn't access that more rational plane of thinking. And deep down I knew he was right.

I suspected Shane knew about me, even before that night. A growing hostility had punctured our interactions. Whenever I wingmanned for the finance bros, he eyed me with simmering contempt. I understood this and didn't blame him. I was clinging to a false identity and its attendant privilege, seamlessly passing between two worlds.

The others were already home and playing music in the kitchen. Shane went straight to his room and shut the door.

Ashley cooked burgers in a pan. Kirsten and I opened a tub of vanilla ice cream. Colby filled a Yankees cup with rosé. He started eating chips and getting crumbs all over the floor.

"Colby, are you okay?" asked Perrie.

Colby called her a stupid cunt. His anger was so inexplicable, so clearly the product of an inner volatility, that Perrie shrank back. We all did.

"Something's wrong with you," Perrie said. "Something is wrong and you're not telling anyone. What's wrong, Colby? What's wrong?"

He repeated the vulgar word and wandered into the living room, leaving a trail of Tostitos crumbs across the shag carpet. The approaching end of summer was apparently bringing out the worst in us.

One by one the others went to bed, but I was still hopped up from my tiff with Shane. I went to the porch with my iPod and the Bose speakers, breaking Mike's cardinal rule from the email. I put on my Montauk playlist and took in the night. The pool glowed through the trees.

It was late, probably three a.m., when the door slid open. I turned around, startled. Shane was standing in his lacrosse pinny and board shorts, his hair flattened by a failed attempt at sleep. Stripped of his pastel polos and knitted belts, he appeared more vulnerable. He clutched a lighter, a bowl, and a small bag of weed.

He sat down next to me and silently packed the bowl. I watched as he took a hit and held it. He tilted his head back, letting the smoke putter out of his lips. A minute or two passed. He handed the bowl to me.

Shane and I couldn't have been more different. He was practical, detail-driven, and devoted to structure. I was emotional, creative, and drawn to chaos. He found beauty through the physical arrangement of space. I patrolled it through language. That night, as the bowl passed between us, those differences dissipated. The weed brokered an unspoken reconciliation. Two only children, searching for a way to belong.

———————————

I woke up and scrolled through my phone. An article on CNN.com caught my eye.

MARGARET PELLEGRINI, FLOWERPOT MUNCHKIN IN 'THE WIZARD OF OZ,' DEAD AT 89

I opened up the article. Growing up I'd had a strong affinity with *The Wizard of Oz* and often performed the songs in our basement. I wasn't a theatrical kid, but Dorothy's Technicolor transformation left me moonstruck. The golden lily pads, the purple fountains, the green hills of Munchkinland blooming in colossal frames. I loved the way the Scarecrow flailed around, scattering the Yellow Brick Road with trails of loose hay. Loved the Cowardly Lion's vibratoed "King of the For-r-r-rest."

My mom was a big fan of the movie, too, and we rented it from Blockbuster every week, until one October, for my birthday, I received a VHS copy of my own. My favorite part came at the end, when Dorothy awoke in Kansas, soaked once again in soothing shades of sepia. In her four-poster bed, surrounded by her family, the colors of Oz felt garish.

As I lay in bed I wondered what my mother had thought. Had she known the stereotypes associated with Judy Garland and the gay world, how Dorothy's displacement reflected the dislocation of gay men? If she had any inkling, she never insinuated anything. The movie remained our own shared amulet.

I emailed the story to my mom under the subject line "poor munchkins."

Mike and Shane were going to Bake Shoppe to pick up the cake for Perrie's birthday. It was Funfetti with chocolate frosting. No one, least of all Perrie, would eat it, but Shane cherished the symbolism. Amid our devious swirl of alcohol and drugs, a cake signified stability and tradition. Mike and Shane made Colby join them for the ride.

Halfway to town, Mike pulled off the road. Colby looked confused. His eyes were dry and bloodshot, hair tamed in a black baseball cap. He was not an early riser; he wasn't sure what was happening. All he knew was that he needed to start drinking again.

For the next half hour Mike and Shane berated him. Colby was blacking out every night and alienating housemates. His mood swings were violent and jarring. Multiple people in the house had complained.

"Who are you to talk, Shane? You black out harder than I do."

"Perrie came to us crying this morning," said Mike. "Do you know what you called her last night?"

Colby had no idea. Mike told him.

"You've been combative with pretty much everyone."

Colby hated the person he had become. Some nights he'd get drunk and start crying for no reason. He'd wake up the next morning and wish he were dead. He had planned to come out to his parents that past Christmas, knowing the news would be an adjustment. Then, on December 13, his mom had been diagnosed with stage 4 ovarian cancer.

He never told anyone she was sick. When he wasn't helping her with her recovery he buried himself in work and drank to oblivion. He still hadn't told his parents he was gay. He lived with the constant fear that his mother would die without knowing him.

In the car that morning he began to sob. He was twenty-five. It was all too much. He needed his mother. He needed her well. His life, he realized, was no longer in his control.

Mike got out of the car and joined him in the back seat. He held him for a while and let him cry.

"We'll help you through this. We all will."

For the first time in months, Colby felt something akin to relief. He would talk to Perrie before her party and patch things up. He would begin the slow process of letting people in.

That day at the beach, playing around on my phone, I came across an old article by my younger cousin Jay. As kids we spent hours playing basketball together, and now Jay worked as a sports journalist and Celtics beat writer for the *Springfield Republican*. In April he had written a piece on Jason Collins, a former center for the Celtics and the first professional basketball player to come out as gay. I angled my screen and began to read.

"What do I hope happens to Jason Collins?" Jay wrote. "I want him to land on an NBA roster because he earned it with hard work and professionalism. I want him to find thorough happiness now that he doesn't have to hide his sexuality. I want others to accept him regardless of who he's attracted to. I want him to hear the ignorant detractors, let their words brush by him without any impact whatsoever and keep his head held high."

In my head I could hear my cousin Jay's voice. He was speaking these words directly to me. I buried my head in my beach towel so that no one could see me cry.

Later that afternoon, at the beach, Mike had his own breakdown. He asked me to go for a walk to Ditch Plains. He was seriously considering breaking up with Shane. He wanted to admit his feelings to Parker and see where things might lead. Part of me believed this was a good idea. I'd watched his relationship with Shane grow increasingly toxic, and felt a break might do them both some good.

"My heart's just constantly hurting for Parker," he said. "I've never felt this way before. I love him."

"You've never felt this way for Shane before?"

"No. Which is why I don't trust it. What if this is just an infatuation? What if it fades?"

We stopped at the Ditch Witch cart for ice cream sandwiches, watching the surfers floating in the waves. I understood Mike's predicament. I'd spent that whole summer constantly questioning my own reality, unable to decipher truth from fantasy. Slowly we began the long walk back.

Night came, and the entire house congregated in the kitchen for flip cup to celebrate Perrie's birthday. We filled the Hive cups with thumbfuls of beer, watching them smack the table, the foam pooling between the cans. I played throwbacks on my iPod: Nelly, Backstreet Boys, and TLC. Cup after cup, spinning through the air, landing on the table upside down.

We were tan and energized and singing along to all the songs on my playlist. We felt young. Perrie was dancing like she did as a kid, arms extended, legs swaying, red hair flowing down her delicate shoulders. The pregame was always better than the party itself.

Chapter Twenty

On Thursday, August 29, Kirsten and Ashley went to Bounce, a high-end sports bar in the Flatiron District with TVs in metal cages. The scene was frenetic—an aggressive whirl of frat stars, spendthrifts, sexy service workers, rappers, and fathers from the 'burbs about to miss their train.

"I got our first round," Ashley said, starting a tab. Kirsten was low on funds and the security deposit for their new apartment was due. In two weeks they'd be moving from Alphabet City to a smaller apartment in SoHo.

Kirsten was looking forward to a fresh start. Her life was not where she wanted it to be. She was going out every night, bingeing on McDonald's, sleeping through her alarm, slinking into work in oversize sunglasses, powering through her copywriting, fighting to maintain a façade of composure. On the nights she stayed in, she suffered insomnia. She didn't exercise and didn't care. She'd stopped caring about anything. After work, when they went out together, Ashley's eye-catching perfection only heightened Kirsten's insecurity. Ashley's presence, down to the Jack Rogers flats and strewn bandage dresses that spangled their living room, was inescapable.

At the bar they bumped into Rivers, a Montauk friend and former Notre Dame cornerback. He was the male equivalent of Ashley, a known and beloved presence within our extended network. His share house often set up camp next to ours on the beach.

"It's gonna be packed this weekend," he said. "I don't know how our house will fit everyone. Honestly, I can't wait for the summer to be over."

"What?" Ashley blinked. "No!"

"It's been a nightmare. We've had so much drama. Our house is always a mess. No one's willing to help out. There's so much infighting. Is the Hive like that?"

"Actually, no," Ashley said. "It's dramatic for sure, but we keep the house clean. Everyone contributes."

"Well, you guys are the exception. I'm only going out there because it's the last weekend. I'm over it."

Kirsten tapped her glass to Rivers's Bud Light. "You and me both."

Kirsten got home that night, drunk, and emailed Stefano a long, heartfelt missive. Their fraught connection carried a dark allure akin to the billowing clouds of a thunderstorm.

Kirsten was drawn to shadow. She conflated pain with emotional depth and instinctively avoided healthy coping mechanisms. Like many people in the Hive, myself included, she was hardwired for self-destruction—attracted to the unstable, the impermeable, the emotionally unavailable. She had hoped that summer would disrupt the cycle, but it hadn't. If anything it had accelerated it. She had not found love in Montauk, or even real romance. She had not come any closer to finding herself.

I packed my bag that night in under ten minutes. Two bone-thin pastel T-shirts, a Saturdays bathing suit, a pair of dark-washed jeans that I chose because Matt had complimented them. A white linen shirt and short-sleeve gingham button-down, one nice pair of high-seamed khaki shorts, Champion workout shorts, Gap boxers, two pairs of Nike running socks, cell phone charger, iPod cord, Dopp kit. Outside, the early tints of fall glimmered through the window. Twilight seemed bluer, more vivid. The old trees in Duane Park were beginning to turn. I could've slept without my air conditioner that night, but doing so would have signaled an end. I wasn't ready for summer to be over.

My Friday routine was burnished with nostalgia. I left my cubicle at one p.m. sharp, rode the 7 to Hunter's Point, purchased an iced coffee, and found a window seat in the last train car. Passing through the familiar stops, I turned on my iPod, the songs merging with my conflicted emotions. I took in the blurred landmarks. Geometric neighborhoods, sand-blown parking lots, the water tower at Hampton Bays, signs for East Hampton, a golf course at the stop for Amagansett. As the train passed Cyril's fish shack, I hovered off my seat. I was crossing into Montauk for the last time.

Through a stand of trees, the bay swept into view, its docks and boats bathed in cloud-struck light. I thought of all the selves I'd been, all the selves I would become. I would never return to Montauk as this person. As the train slowed into the station, I didn't look back.

The Montauket was one of the last holdouts of Old Montauk, a seaside motel crusted with buoys, painted driftwood, and steel-

blue clapboards. It hugged a rocky hill on the Sound, impermeable to change, a barnacle. When evening fell, the sun sank into
the Sound in wavering layers, painting the sky above the Montauket in luminous, cloud-ripped sediments.

A live band was performing on the grass-fringed patio. As the
sun dipped down everyone trained their eyes to the horizon. People took photos, raised glasses, and cheered. Ashley and I went
inside to the bar.

"What are you drinking?" she asked.

"Painkiller."

She turned to the bartender. "Two more Painkillers."

I took out my wallet but she slapped it away.

"How are you? How's your heart? Have you been following
my instructions?"

I nodded. To Ashley, love was a sport complete with strategies
and playbooks. For the past week she had been coaching me. I
was not to text or Gchat Matt unless he messaged first. If he did
text, I had to keep my answers friendly but short. In a group setting I needed to be effusively upbeat and engaging to everyone
around me but him.

"When he gets to Montauk tomorrow, you need to be aloof.
Act like you're not excited to see him. If you pull away slightly,
he'll come for you. I guarantee it. It's the law of attraction."

Matt had a wedding in the city that night. He was driving out
the next morning with his best friend Kelley, the one he'd told
me about on the roof. She was staying in a different house, but
Matt had wanted me to meet her.

Can't wait to see you tomorrow!!! he texted me.

Same, I texted back.

The night unfolded as expected. Ruschmeyer's, Point and Mem, Pizza Village, Hive. When Kirsten woke up the next morning, Ashley had already worked out and showered.

"Which is best?" Ashley asked, holding up two bikini tops. "The blue or the frill?"

"Blue."

The dread Kirsten felt as she awoke was unlike any she'd ever known. She had slaked herself into a stupor the night before and drunk-texted both Nick Tot and Stefano. She felt pathetic.

"I was a mess last night."

"Oh my God, you were not! I'd tell you."

"I was. I scared away Nick Tot and then I drunk-texted him." She reached for her phone on the bedside table, but Ashley placed it out of reach.

"Kirsten, *forget* Nick Tot!" She unhooked her bikini top. "It's a beautiful day, we're gonna meet *new* boys!" A new bikini held aloft. "I'm single this weekend, so are you, and we're gonna find *hot* guys, and it's gonna be amazing. We'll be outgoing, we'll look killer. Forget about last night. Who cares if they didn't text you back? We're gonna meet. *New*. Boys."

That day, after a lap through the Tuna, we hopped in a cab bound for Cyril's fish shack. At the outdoor bar two blond bartenders were dropping whole bananas into a row of blenders, mixing in rum, milk, liqueur, and Kahlua to make batches of BBCs.

"This. Is. Insane," said Ashley as we made our way through the dining room. Waitresses in CYRIL'S SAYS RESPECT tees were ferrying lobster rolls and fried clams. A line for the bathroom ran down the hall and out the door. Cyril himself sat at a round table in the corner. He had long white hair, a white beard, red-rimmed glasses, and a straw hat. He tapped his cigarette into a full ashtray next to a stack of paperback thrillers. Amid the bacchanal he was a sphinxlike presence, rarely talking and never moving from his sun-drenched station.

Ashley went up to him and kissed him on the cheek. "It's the last weekend. Do you mind if we take a picture with you?" She and Kirsten posed on the arms of his chair.

We walked to the back parking lot, where the picnic tables had been cleared for dancing. A train whipped by, not thirty yards away. It whistled at the crowd, dispersed a cold rush of air. Everyone cheered.

"Hey, over here!" Mike called to a waitress with BBCs. "Can we get, like, the whole tray?"

"Hell yeah." The waitress nodded. "Twelve each."

She rested her tray on a nearby table and we handed her our cash. "BBC-ya later," Mike said as he picked up a drink with a thick rum floater. I raised my cup and drank, the buttery sweet banana liqueur mixing with the sharpness of the rum.

We joked that we only came to Cyril's to drink milk in a hot parking lot, but that was pretty much what we were doing, and hundreds of others were doing the same. Around us dance circles were forming, beach scarves stretching into impromptu limbo sticks. Kelsey O'Brian started to twerk against a plastic trash can. Guys bought rosé by the bottle, then raced between cars to piss discreetly.

Dueling bachelorette parties were vying for Timmy's attention as DJ Biggie de Black Rhino played a set of remixes beneath his bright blue tent. There were always bachelorette parties at Cyril's, and Timmy's favorite activity was to dance-battle with the bride-to-be.

I finished my BBC and switched to beer. I was spirited but distracted, the end of the summer suffusing the party with a strange, sad urgency, like the last night of college.

As I made my way through the parking lot, I saw Matt.

He wore a white V-neck tee, backward cap, and blue floral bathing suit. He looked road-weary but happy. I steeled myself as I approached, remembering what Ashley had instructed me.

"Hey!" He went in for a hug and I stayed rigid. He pulled back, eyeing me quizzically. "How are you?"

"I'm good."

"That's good. Kelley just dropped me off. She's unpacking at her friend's share. I'm so tired from the wedding. We all went to Pier A after. Have you ever been there?"

"Once or twice."

"How was last night?"

"Good."

"That's good."

I turned away. "Mike, did Caroline text you about the bonfire?"

"Maybe. I don't know. I'm not getting any service right now."

"I know!" Matt jumped in. "I tried calling you both, like, a dozen times." He looked at me as he said this. "I just assumed you'd be here."

I held his gaze for a moment, then turned away. "Oh, look, Mike, there's Sarah and Mallory! Let's go say hi to them."

As I pulled Mike toward two of our college friends, I looked back at Matt, catching the confusion in his pale blue eyes. Almost instantly I felt guilty. Did he know what I was doing? Could he see through my frostiness? Did he intuit the correlation between his relationship and my misery?

The sun-bleached crowd dissolved around me. Hundreds of people laughing and dancing, animated by the shared privilege of the milieu. The intoxicating swirl sharpened my despair. I could have Matt as a friend or not at all. Both options made me want to die.

I sat in the Land Rover holding a bag of Jet-Puffed marshmallows. In the truck were blankets, extra chairs, and stacks of firewood. It was dark, the car was full, and we were driving toward the beach.

"Guys, I'm so sad. I like, can't. Oh my God, look at the moon, it's so beautiful. Everything about tonight is perfect, especially all of you."

The glow of the crescent moon illuminated Ashley's tears. Mike was sitting shotgun. "Jesus, Ash! I haven't even put on Coldplay yet. Save some feelings for the rest of us."

She smiled and wiped the tears from her eyes. "Stop. You guys are my family."

"I barely tolerate any of you," Shane said.

"I'm too dead inside to feel anything," I joked.

"What if the car flipped right now, like in season three of *The OC*?" Mike asked. "Which one of us would be the Marissa?"

"Mike, don't speak ill of the dead!" Kirsten shouted, laughing.

"Marissa Cooper had a great thigh gap," Colby said.

"Remember when she shot Trey?" said Perrie.

In unison the entire car started singing the chorus to the Imogen Heap song that played when Marissa Cooper shot Trey in a season two cliffhanger episode. We watched Mike's full-season DVDs whenever it rained.

"I think I'm Julie Cooper," Mike said as we pulled into the Sloppy Tuna parking lot. "I'm quick-witted, a redhead, and good at exploiting those around me."

"I'm Ryan Atwood in a kimono!" shouted Colby.

"Kirsten is Kirsten!"

"Parker is Ryan Atwood because he's our guest."

"Parker is *not* Ryan Atwood."

"Hey! I could be Ryan Atwood!"

"You're too nice, though."

"Yeah, Ryan has an edge."

"What about Sandy Cohen?"

"I'd fuck Sandy Cohen!"

The conversation ended just in time.

On the beach we joined forces with Everett's house. Everett and D.Lo's relationship had blossomed over the past two months. Each Saturday they'd abscond to Ditch Plains, buy ice cream at the Ditch Witch truck, and walk the coast. The dunes were high and crumbling and chocolate brown, and they cradled the sea. Everett would surf while D.Lo read. Then they'd rejoin the group in time for Cyril's.

We'd become good friends with Everett and his housemates. Most of them were single and all of them were straight. A natural affinity coalesced between them and the Hive girls. Perrie especially.

"I've slept with half the people at this bonfire," she whispered to me, covering her head with her shawl.

213

We roasted marshmallows and pressed them into s'mores. It reminded me of my family's childhood trips to Camp Holy Cross, a parish campground in the Berkshires. During the day we swam in the pond and played kickball in an unkempt field. We stayed in cabins without plumbing or electricity and made our meals—hot dogs, Dinty Moore beef stew, and s'mores—on an open fire. I had a fear of fire but tried to be brave. I remember my aunt Trisha cradling me. *You're safe. We're all safe. Nothing can hurt you.*

Shane had purchased paper lanterns at White's Drug Store. I watched the lanterns catch and rise to the sky, each a silent prayer. It was a windy night and they ascended quickly, disappearing into the stars.

The night was wistful and emotionally charged. Ashley could not stop crying. I too was on the cusp of tears, the summer returning to me in Kodachrome slides. I had believed, in my late twenties, that I was beyond the point of making so many new friends. The Hive had created an opening. The Hive had brought me Matt.

I heard him calling my name through the merriment. He was approaching with a beautiful girl. His knuckles were rolled into the sleeves of his green hoodie.

"John, this is my friend Kelley."

She gave me a strong hug, and I took in her delicate glamour. She had a thin frame, porcelain skin, boat-swept blond hair. The blue-and-white striped sweater wrapped around her shoulders reminded me of New England. Nothing about her suggested she was physically unwell. If anything she exuded a strong-willed vitality. I was incapable of viewing her in any other light.

"It's nice to meet you," she said. "I've heard so much about you."

In the glow of the fire I caught a defiant spark in her eye. As we spoke it became clear that she cherished Matt, but she looked like the kind of friend who collared no bullshit. I wondered what they had talked about on their long car ride from the city. I wondered what she knew about me, or thought she knew. She seemed to treat Matt with the perfect balance of gravity and whimsy. But I sensed, in our brief exchange, that she was on my side, too.

Near the end of the night, Mike and Parker stole away. They carried their drinks to the tideline and watched the last of the paper lanterns floating by. They started talking, their voices getting lost in the loud crash of the waves.

"What'd you say?"

"What's that?"

"Huh?"

They leaned in closer until all they could see was the whites of their teeth.

When no one was watching, their lips met.

It was our last full day in Montauk. Over the summer the Hive had housed many guests, and each had paid a guest fee of $150 a night. An exception was made for the unanticipated. If you were lucky enough to meet someone at the Mem, they could spend the night for free.

Colby had managed the budget diligently. Between rent deposits and guest fees, we never had to pay for alcohol or groceries, and we were occasionally permitted to use house funds for pizza. By the end of the summer we had enough money in the pot to buy a table at Surf Lodge and to each receive a forty-dollar reimbursement.

"That's a free class at Barry's Bootcamp!" squealed Timmy. We had spent the morning at the beach and were back at the house playing beer pong. Some of the girls were upstairs getting ready. Our reservation at Surf Lodge was for three p.m.

"I'm obsessed with Barry's," said Matt. "It's so hard, I die every time." He took wobbly aim at the cups and missed by a mile. He was already pretty drunk. Since the bonfire the night before, I had abandoned Ashley's protocol. I didn't see the point in pretending to be aloof or disinterested in Matt with one day left. He was the source of all my emotional turbulence, but his mere proximity made me feel whole. It was a vicious paradox that, at twenty-seven, I was coming to know for the first time.

Kelley took aim at the cups. She had gravitated to the mellower of the Hive girls—Taylor, Dana, and Kara—and the three of them had gotten ready together. "Guys, I'm like, nervous for the Surf Lodge. I hear everyone's evil there."

"I mean, to be fair, everyone's evil here." Timmy waved his hands to signal the whole house. "But the Surf Lodge is like that quasi-abusive high school coach who screams at you during practice and makes you do extra wind sprints and tells you you're worthless. It makes your life hell, but it's oddly motivating."

We nodded in agreement.

The entire house packed into Henry's cab. I sat in the way back with Matt and Kelley, knees tucked to my chest, my Solo cup jostling. The cops were out in full force that weekend, so Henry dropped us off a hundred yards from the Surf Lodge to avoid drawing their attention.

"Leave your empty cups in here," he instructed. "Someone got a fifteen-hundred-dollar ticket for littering the other weekend. I don't want my bees going bankrupt."

We walked on the roadside between the parked cars and the guardrail. To our left the pond stretched like a plate of flat glass. A vast bullpen had already formed at the entrance, and we attempted to slide through the crowds to the reservations line. Girls in crop tops and fedoras leaned against the divide, waving at the managers with bangled arms.

"Reservations only. No one else is getting in."

A waitress delivered us to an L-shaped day bed in the sand. We kicked off our shoes and sprawled across the plush yellow cushions. Colby took charge.

"Two buckets of Dos Equis, a bottle of Whispering Angel, a carafe of Endless Summer, and a bottle of Grey Goose. Oh, and a bucket of chicken fingers."

I looked over the menu as Colby pointed. The chicken finger bucket was eighty-five dollars.

"We're treatin' ourselves today. Dad's gotta make sure his Hive kids eat well!"

The sun was strong, but a breeze skimmed off the pond. Hipsters, socialites, and new-media wunderkinds circulated the deck with practiced ennui, but the vibe on the sand was ethereal and relaxed. We people-watched, taking in the bohemian opulence of the scene. One of our favorite games was to sort people into the houses from *Harry Potter*. We spent hours doing this on the beach and endlessly argued about what houses we ourselves belonged to. The vast majority of the Surf Lodge that day was Slytherin.

"What about him?" Mike nodded to a broad-shouldered guy in a T-shirt and khaki shorts. "He could be Gryffindor. He's even wearing red." The guy had a smooth face, angled jaw, and oak eyes. He looked wholesome and innocent. Just then he produced a small bag of coke and snorted some off the top of his hand.

"Ten points for Slytherin."

Thoughts of Harry Potter carried me back to Longmeadow, to those bleary-eyed nights of addictive reading, to the books I carried each summer in my backpack. In high school my cousin Jay and I lifeguarded at Bliss Pool, the public facility in our hometown. On rest breaks I'd sneak into the guard house, devouring *The Poisonwood Bible*, *Catch-22*, *Beloved*, the stories of Flannery O'Connor.

One day, a storm swept in, clearing the pool of swimmers before abruptly dissipating. With Bliss to ourselves, we all walked to the deep end, where a twelve-foot-tall lifeguard chair stood between the diving boards. One by one I watched as the veteran guards scaled the chair, then jumped—whooping and screaming as they plunged toward the water. When it was my turn, I climbed the thick rungs and stood for a second, absorbed in the vertigo of my vantage. From that old wooden perch I could see everything—the fields I had run through as a child, the trees I'd climbed, the swings I'd attempted to flip over the bar, and the basketball court where I'd played countless games of Knockout. Then, before I could think too much, before I could talk myself out of it, I jumped.

"Where's the bathroom?" Matt asked. He was bombed and had to break the seal. The Surf Lodge men's room had one enclosed stall and a urinal trough that could accommodate two people at most. The line extended from the barn to the patio. At the edge of the sand stood an old-fashioned projector screen framed by a wall of dense shrubs.

"Just go behind the projector," said Kirsten. "No one will see you."

"I need to go, too," said Shane. "And I am *not* waiting in that line."

Matt and Shane stumbled through the maze of day beds. I watched as they indiscreetly knocked into the projector screen before walking around it. The moment they finished relieving themselves, a security guard with iron-clad biceps escorted them out. They drunkenly lingered in the parking lot before stumbling into a cab. Kelley didn't know what to do.

"I feel bad. I should go back."

"Honestly, I'm so exhausted from the sun," said Dana. "I'll go back with you once I finish my drink."

"I haven't seen Matt this drunk since college." Kelley started to laugh. "It's kinda hysterical."

I asked her what Matt was like in college. As close as we were, I had a hard time envisioning his social scene.

"We met at a Halloween party freshman year," Kelley said. "Matt had just rushed a frat. He was dressed as Peter Pan. It was, like, the perfect costume for him. He had this innocence about him. Céline Dion started to play and we bonded."

"Was he out freshman year?"

"No. But Céline Dion saved us the conversation. You've heard the Tucker story, right?"

"No. Who's Tucker?"

She winced, and I noticed her Miraculous Medal. It dangled from a thin gold chain.

"Tucker was Matt's first love," she confided. "He was the first person to break his heart."

I stood there, blank-faced, synthesizing the story. Matt had fallen in love with his best friend from college. They'd met at freshman orientation and started hooking up first semester, always in secret. During winter break, they'd sleep over at each other's houses, and their parents had no clue. Their relationship continued into sophomore year. Matt wanted more. He wanted them to be together openly. When he voiced this desire, Tucker started pulling away. He claimed he wasn't gay and would never have a relationship with a guy. Matt was destroyed.

"Pretty soon after that he came out to me," Kelley said.

As the sun set over Fort Pond a live band took to the stage. Ashley started crying again, and Mike did, too. Time stretched to accommodate a strange celestial energy. Timmy had passed out across the day bed.

"Timmy!" Colby shook him. "Come on, honey! You're embarrassing yourself!"

"Mrrrgggh," he mumbled, and rolled over.

"Come on, Timmy. We're all leaving. It's time to go home."

I had done a good job of pacing myself that afternoon, limiting my alcohol intake to an Endless Summer and two beers, padding my stomach with a clutch of overpriced chicken fingers. But something about the short, doleful lull ahead of us—the downtime between dinner and town—shuttled my thoughts down a dark canal. As we dispersed into the Hive's dark corners, I decided to take a shower to wake myself up.

The water streamed down my face and onto the sponge-soft foot mats. In high school I'd ritualized the last shower of summer—a washing away of the scents I associated with fizzy, starlit freedom. Sunblock, bug spray, chlorine, and cheap Keystone beer. I thought about Matt's college love affair. The searing confusion, the fear of rejection, the lonely cage of his feelings—he had been through it already, had built a wall against it. In his current boyfriend he had found Tucker's opposite—a middle-aged millionaire.

How could I convince Matt that I was not Tucker?

On the window ledge stood a phalanx of shampoo bottles, conditioners, and Dove eucalyptus body wash. Peach facial scrubs, balms and ointments, pink Venus razors in plastic holders. I cranked open the window and the air crept in, casting the bathroom in a halo of steam. Throughout the summer we had carried Montauk with us—in the taste of salt, the pink of our noses, the grains of sand embedded in our hair. I had carried other things with me, too, and now I could not carry them anymore. I needed to tell Matt how I felt. I wanted him to know I was different. I wouldn't abandon him. My life had started the moment I met him.

When I turned off the water I could hear the sounds of insects harmonizing in the grass. I was going to talk to him. I was going to reveal my heart.

We got ready that night more out of obligation than anything else. We planned to go to Shagwong, a time-worn watering hole next to Herb's Market on Main Street. Founded in 1969, Shagwong counted Andy Warhol, John Lennon, and the Rolling Stones among its habitués. The wooden walls were scratched and smoke-stained, the ceiling still cast in original plasterwork. Faded sepia photos hung above the lacquered booths where locals ordered the fish of the day. On the weekends Shagwong had live music—cover bands that stuck to the hits. It was the opposite of the Surf Lodge in the best possible way.

I was absorbed in a game of Kings in the Hive's living room when Mike came downstairs.

"Come outside with me."

"Huh?"

"It's important."

He pulled me off the couch and onto the front deck. His eyes were wide and sparkling. I couldn't read him. He looked bubbly, almost manic. I braced myself. Something must have happened with Parker.

"Okay, first off. Promise me you won't be mad."

"Mad about what?"

His face was plastered with a strange grin.

"I told Matt."

I froze, overcome by a sudden hyperawareness: the anxious chirp of crickets, the scent of cigarettes, the touch of the shirt on my biceps, Mike's red hair shadowed in the dark. He continued to speak and I listened through a scrim of adrenaline.

After getting kicked out of Surf Lodge, Matt and Shane had napped until nightfall and were now awake and drinking on the balcony off the bedroom.

"Matt was complaining about his new guy and how he travels all the time. The age difference is taking its toll. I asked him what he thought of you. It just came out, I didn't even mean to—"

"What did he say?"

"He didn't say anything. He had this hesitation in his voice. So I told him how you had feelings for him."

My stomach tightened. "Then what?"

"He has feelings for you, too. It's mutual. He said he likes you. He asked if I thought your feelings for him were real. I said one hundred percent."

I was overcome with a wave of delirium. A cosmic euphoria. I'd devoted every waking thought to him. Every song lyric grafted to his existence. It was real. I wasn't making it up. It was real.

"So then what? Where did you leave it?"

"He said he has to think about it. He felt he had to make a decision."

"About me? About his relationship?"

"Yes."

"He's still upstairs? I need to talk to him—"

"Not yet. Give him at least a night. I don't want him to think I immediately relayed all this to you, even though of course I did."

"I can't believe this is happening. It's not in my head."

"There's no one who deserves it more."

I had no time to process. The moment Mike and I walked back into the living room, Matt came tumbling down the stairs. He walked right up to me and grabbed my hands.

"Hi!" His eyes sparked in a new way.

"Hey! You made a comeback!" We were holding hands, our grip radiating intensity.

"Cabs ah hee-ya!" called Dana, imitating Pauly D from *Jersey Shore*. "We can't keep Henry waiting on our last night!"

In the back row of Henry's cab I had my arm around him. His hand rested on my leg. This was how we rode the whole way to town.

Shagwong was crowded and hot and bathed in red-filtered light. Our friends from other houses were already there. Matt grabbed my hand and guided me to the bar. He ordered us both Blue Moons.

My memories of that night are vivid and impressionistic. The band was set up in front, by the windows. Shagwong had a bar on one side and a restaurant on the other, and on the bar side everyone was dancing. Matt handed me a foaming beer. We did not leave each other's side.

The band started playing "Mr. Brightside." It was one of my favorite songs from college. The whole house swarmed together, jumping up and down, shouting the lyrics. Matt and I were dancing, a part of the group but separate from it, ensconced in our own unspoken world. Everyone in the house must've sensed what was happening. I felt only a sweeping wave of relief. I remember thinking this was the happiest I had ever been.

When we got home I was completely wired. It seemed the whole house had caught a second wind. We ate pizza and danced around the kitchen. Timmy started grinding like a male stripper and Kelley became his objet d'art.

We decided to go skinny-dipping. Mike, Parker, Shane, Timmy, Matt, and me. I hunted through the house for a dry towel and brought down the speakers.

"Timmy, you're a never-nude," Mike joked as we reached the pool deck. "Your idea of skinny-dipping is swimming in long underwear."

"I am *not* a never-nude!" Timmy tossed away his shirt and kicked off his shorts. "What a terrible thing to call someone." He stepped onto the diving board naked and raised his arms to the sky. "Kelley, grade my front flip on a scale of one to ten."

We did naked cannonballs, naked backflips, rode naked down the slide. A primal giddiness charged the air. I stared into the canopy of trees illuminated by watery light, spotting stars through the branches. We stuck to the shadows, strategically covered ourselves with our hands. There was nothing sexual about it. It felt like freedom.

Matt kept playing "Applause" over and over.

"Matt, not again!" Kelley sat by the pool house, taking in our antics.

"Just the chorus! Just the clapping part! Then we can listen to something else."

We were back in the kitchen, just Matt and me. Our hair was wet, but we had changed into dry clothes. Everyone else had gone to bed.

"Wanna keep listening to music?" he asked.

I handed him my iPod and the speakers. He put on a Rihanna's "Do Ya Thang." We moved closer. My arms wrapped around his waist and his arms rested on my shoulders. His back was against the counter and we held each other. I could smell the vodka on his breath. I had sobered up, but he was still drunk. He rested his head on my shoulder.

It was like my body had unlocked a new level of perception. The lightest touch was a live wire, electrifying new dimensions of consciousness. The physical and emotional had never coalesced for me with such intensity.

Matt looked up from my shoulder. We started leaning in. Our foreheads touched. I closed my eyes. We were on the verge of kissing. I had envisioned this countless times, had prayed for it each morning on my walk to the subway. We were as still as Roman statues. We did not speak. I was about to lean in. Then the thought. He was drunk and had a boyfriend. I'd be his point of guilt. I wanted to kiss him more than anything. But I knew that this was not the time. This was not the way.

Knowing it could've happened was enough. This is what I convinced myself. A cold pastoral.

Chapter Twenty-One

It was early, around eight a.m., and no one else was awake. In the dark of Bedroom 4, I hunted for my bathing suit. I walked barefoot back down to the pool. Everything was quiet and still.

I stood at the edge of the diving board, bouncing up and down, the sun striking my body in buckshots of yellow light. This pool, which we'd hardly used, felt like a synaptic bridge, a portal to past selves. Fiberglass diving board, netless basketball hoop, a concrete deck capped with white filters. It reminded me of the long afternoons I spent with my cousins at my aunt Bootsie's pool, pretending we were in the Olympics. On the ride out to Bootsie's we would beg whichever aunt was driving to turn on the car's heat and roll up all the windows. We wanted to get as hot and sweaty as possible, to torture ourselves. That way, when we finally dove into the pool, we'd have truly earned it. We'd sit in the back of the car, bodies stuck to the leather, feeling the wet film on each other's hands. Time stretched and the pain united us as we anticipated the pool's cold release.

I felt my grandmother's presence in the slant of the sun. At Bootsie's pool Kicki timed our handstands and graded our cannonballs. Wrinkled hands washing our scrapes with Bacitracin. Her final gift had brought me to this moment. I was in the Hive because of her. This nascent happiness, this hope, this new life, was because of her.

Shane and I went to the Bake Shoppe for one last jelly croissant. We poured milk through the domed lids of our iced coffee cups and listened to Yacht's "Second Summer" one last time. When we got back to the house, the energy had shifted. Everyone was gathering the remains of their summer lives. Trash bins filled with unsalvageable items—cheap H&M bracelets, overstretched tank tops, a broken pair of Jack Rogers sandals. People passed through the house like ghosts, silent and monofocused. The anxiety was contagious.

Matt brought his duffel bag to the living room. He looked hungover—eyes bagged and skin ashen. "Have you seen my green sweatshirt?" he asked me.

"I think it's on a chair in the kitchen."

"Oh, good. I was so drunk last night I thought I might've worn it out and lost it. I barely remember anything after Surf Lodge."

His words threw me. "Last night was nuts." I laughed nervously.

"Totally."

I scanned his gaze, trying to discern the truth.

Lost and found items accumulated on the kitchen table. Black Tory Burch flats, Mardi Gras beads, a Sonicare electric toothbrush, one Rainbow sandal, a neon orange windbreaker, bottles of Aleve, a tennis racket, two different blue striped bikini tops, gold hoop earrings, La Mer moisturizing cream, a battered copy of *Gone Girl*, New Balance running sneakers, a tangled pile of cell phone chargers, and sweatshirts from Air + Speed.

Ashley went for one last run and rewarded herself with a cigarette on the upstairs deck. She looked down at the driveway, our housemates loading the cars. Perrie's was already pulling away. Ashley would miss her Montauk family. But she had a second date planned that night with Sloppy Tuna Man. They were going to a wine bar on West Fourth Street. She had accomplished what she'd set out to do.

I packed my bag in the dim light of Bedroom 4. I had spent all summer living out of my duffel, never once folding my clothes into a Hive dresser. I wanted the comfort of mobility, the safety of quick escape.

The door creaked open and Matt stepped in.

"Hey," he said.

"Hey."

"I'm doing a load of laundry."

"Oh, smart."

The laundry room was connected to Bedroom 4. He walked past me and unhinged the latched door. I could hear him moving his clothes from the washing machine to the dryer. I followed him in.

"Hey," I said. "Can we talk?"

He tossed in the last of his clothes and mixed in two dryer sheets.

"Of course."

My hands were shaking. My heart stammered. The back of

my throat went dry. Every insecurity I'd ever harbored was rising and crushing me, fracturing my thoughts. I forced myself to speak.

"I know Mike talked to you last night and I just wanted you to know that everything he said was true."

"Oh, yeah. Thank you, I appreciate that."

"I have feelings for you. I really like you. I know you're seeing someone, but I feel like we have such a strong connection."

"I agree."

"Obviously this is new terrain for me. But I know myself and I know how I feel."

"I appreciate that. It takes courage to articulate that. And to be honest, I have feelings for you, too."

No one had ever said those words to me. Not in a way that I could hear. They filled me with deep currents of joy. A lifetime of feeling out of step. Everything now aligned.

"I think you're the best," he continued. "I tell everyone how awesome you are. Kelley loves you."

"She's great. I love her, too."

"And if I weren't in my current relationship I'd totally want to see where things led."

A sudden change, the gears shifting. This was a different conversation. This was obliterating. As he continued to speak I felt myself being whisked away.

"But I really like this new person. I know our connection is real, but there's a big difference between having feelings and being out with them."

I was five and holding Kicki's hand. We were walking along the tide line at Hawk's Nest Beach in Connecticut. She spotted a green shard of sea glass wedged between belts of seaweed. I picked it up and held it in my palm.

"These feelings are new for you and you're still figuring everything out."

The sea glass was curved and luminous. Kicki told me it came from the neck of a bottle. We were walking to an amalgamated rock at the end of the beach. We had all left the cottages together, but Kicki and I had fallen behind. I could see the silhouettes of my cousins against the sun.

"I've been there. It's a lot to process, but it's something everyone has to sort through and it takes time. I can be your friend and help you through it, but I can't be your coach."

The sea glass cast a green shadow across Kicki's golf shirt. She asked me if I thought it was ready. True sea glass was tide-battered and sunbaked. Ossified and parched and dried up by salt. Swept against rocks and hard shells. The harshness made it softer. Its edges became smooth and opaque. In my head the bottleneck was already mine. I pictured it next to the little things atop my dresser: my neon snap bracelet, my California Raisin figurine, my bamboo case of baby teeth.

"I'm not looking for a coach," I said. "You're not an experiment. I know we're at different stages, but I know I want to be with you. I'm not afraid of how I feel."

I knew the sea glass wasn't ready. The edges were still too sharp. But I wanted it. Kicki understood. She had her own little things atop her dresser, and boxes and boxes of things in the attic. Once, when I was little, I explored her trove with my cousin Carly, opening boxes and cedar chests and sifting through costume jewelry and yearbooks and the loose fabric of my grandfather's World War II parachute. The adults saw what we had done and yelled at us. Not Kicki, though. Kicki never once yelled or got mad.

"The timing isn't right. You'll see. Who knows what can happen down the road."

Seeing the anguish on my face, Kicki quickly scanned the beach around us. *Johnny*, she said, and pointed.

There, lying in the sand, was another piece of sea glass. It glowed an indigo blue. Back in Springfield Kicki had jars and jars of sea glass that she'd take down and let me play with. In all her years of collecting she had only ever found one other piece that was blue.

I scooped it up and dusted the sand off. Kicki told me the blue was the rarest of them all and that it was mine.

"Okay. Obviously I'm disappointed, but I understand," I said. "I'm glad we talked."

"Me too."

On our way back to the cottage, Kicki let me toss the bottleneck back to the sea. It was an offering for another day, another beach, another year. The sky was clear and Kicki pointed across the Sound. I didn't know it then, but she was pointing directly to Montauk.

WINTER

Chapter Twenty-Two

It was already setting out to be one of the coldest winters on record. Just after the new year a nor'easter struck, pummeling the city with arctic winds and whorls of snow. The temperature in Central Park plunged to four degrees Fahrenheit, breaking a previous low set in 1896. At night, Chauvin, Evan, and I set up a space heater on the coffee table and huddled around as we watched the news. The weathermen were calling it a polar vortex.

As the cold front persisted, I found myself longing for summer. I pictured our beach camp on the other side of the volleyball nets, the days that were too hot to do anything but body surf. I yearned for those humid, buzzy nights when, in T-shirts and shorts, we'd drink vodka sodas outside the Mem. These nostalgic echoes of Montauk initially caught me off guard. The emotional fallout from the Hive had been almost too much to bear.

Labor Day weekend had left me cratered. I'd revealed my feelings to Matt and exposed a part of my inner life I was just coming to understand. Returning to the city in disarray, I'd retreated inside myself. I felt simultaneously unmasked and invisible. I had no idea how to continue to live my life.

I walked to the subway each morning fighting back tears, praying to my grandmother just to make it through the day. I remember weaving through the underground concourse beneath my building the Wednesday after Labor Day, lost in the sunless glow of shops and restaurants. I got in line at a salad shop. Who knows what I ordered. Even the simplest act of getting lunch had become alien and humiliating. Amid the winding ropes of people, I felt exposed, unlovable, and deeply pathetic. I had risked everything for a chance at real intimacy. It hadn't worked out. In my own interior world I no longer felt welcome.

That night I texted my mom. I asked her if I could come home for the weekend. I explained that I was feeling sad and overwhelmed. I was suffering the worst heartache of my life. She told me not to take the train all the way home. She'd meet me halfway and pick me up in New Haven.

On the Metro-North that Friday I took in the landscape. The city had faded to oceanfront suburbs—Greenwich McMansions with blue lawns and boat docks. I pictured the families that lived in those houses, their life paths replicated over and over. I wanted to replicate that same path, too. I wondered now if I ever would.

I found both my parents outside Union Station. My dad had gotten out of work early and decided to join my mom for the trip. I tossed my canvas bag in his trunk.

"I'm so glad we get you for the whole weekend," my mom said as she kissed me.

After twenty minutes of compulsory small talk, the conversation shifted inward.

"So," my mom asked. "How are you?"

I tried to speak but couldn't. A heat was rising through my chest. I had kept it in all week, bottled my pain.

I admitted I had had my heart broken. I realized I was crying.

"Johnny, I know you're in pain, but it'll be okay. You'll find someone soon. Trust me."

"No, you don't understand." I was too emotionally decimated, too sleep-deprived and mentally burdened to even consider what I was about to say. "My heart was broken by a guy."

The car veered, a horn blasted. The steering wheel whiplashed back into place.

"Phil?" my mom said. "Phil, are you okay?"

"No," my dad said. "No, I'm not okay. I need to pull over."

My dad took the nearest exit and pulled into an empty factory parking lot. He stopped the car.

"Get out."

I stepped onto the asphalt, completely numb. My dad walked over to me. He gave me the strongest hug I had ever received.

The rest of the weekend was triage. I didn't know at the time whether I was gay or bi, but I was beginning to believe that my capacity for romantic love might be much greater with a man. My parents were shocked but supportive, and we spent the weekend processing what my feelings meant, for me and for them. As we sat on the patio they peppered me with questions. *Did you ever like girls?* Yes, but not with the same intensity. *Do you want to be romantic with a guy?* Yes, I do. *Could this just be a one-off?* I don't think so. *What do you think you'll do next?* Call us a pizza.

I could see how my confession was dismantling the future

they'd conceived for me—a vision that predated my existence, a fantasy that had germinated in the earliest sparks of their own relationship. But during that weekend, and the weeks to come, they were there for me.

We will ALWAYS be your loving and supportive parents no matter what, my mom wrote in an email. We love you and the person you are. I couldn't have asked for a better son.

Despite their support, I could sense, over the next few months, that my parents were in mourning. They were grieving for a vision of my life that would no longer be tenable—a relationship and eventual marriage to a woman. Over the course of that fall I had to give them the space to accept me.

Over Gchat I told my cousin Jay. You're my brother and always will be, he typed back right away. This update wasn't even necessary. You deserve awesomeness whether it comes in guy form or girl form.

The process of telling my family validated a truth I knew all along—that they loved me no matter what, that my sexuality didn't define me. Yet as I looped in more cousins, aunts, and uncles, my heart drifted to Kicki and Pop-Pop. I'd never have the chance to tell them my truth. I'd never know how they'd react. They'd never know this capacity within me.

They do, my aunt Trisha said to me over Thanksgiving. *They wanted this for you, and they love you. We all do.*

Even though I was confident they'd be supportive, I was nervous to open up to my friends. As an only child my friendships informed how I moved through the world. I had always surrounded myself with open-minded people, and the rational part of me knew I had nothing to fear. But as I bucked up the courage to talk to my roommates, I felt my palms begin sweat. At work one afternoon I silently counted to ten. Then I counted to three. Then I sent Chauvin a message, asking if we could talk that night.

"This changes nothing," he assured me later on in our apartment. "I'm still going to make fun of you for everything. Most of all I'm sorry you were feeling such heartache. I've been there."

"You should tell everyone," Evan said. "All our friends will be thrilled for you. We all just want you to be happy."

I went to bed that night, my heart thrumming with profound gratitude.

My friends from the Hive were among my biggest supporters. In every single conversation, my sexual identity was secondary to my lovesickness. Everyone was more concerned about how I could heal my heart.

As I gained more distance from the summer, I felt the rustling of an unfamiliar hope. If I could go this deep with Matt, perhaps I could go this deep with other men. The prospect of a meaningful relationship and all that it entailed—a partnership, a home, and, one day, a family—had shifted. But in some ways it now felt even more within reach. The cornerstone of building a family, of raising children, was, of course, love. I had more confidence that I could one day find it in a genuine form.

I saw Matt a couple of times that fall. The mere sight of him catalyzed immense emotional pain. Every time he posted a new photo on Instagram or Facebook I felt physically ill. Ultimately I found a way to keep him at a safe remove without severing our connection. In part I did so by dipping my toes, very gingerly, into my new sexuality. The guys of the Hive took me to my first gay bar, where someone approached me. We talked about *Harry Potter* and Camus and exchanged numbers. He texted me the next day to ask me out. We met for oysters in the East Village and developed a rapport. He was the first guy I was intimate with.

I knew I had more to figure out. But for the first time in a long time I no longer felt breakable. I felt strong.

Epilogue

The snow has started again, and Lonnie the weatherman is projecting two feet. Down in Tribeca the streets are windy. The storm batters against our black windows, but our living room is snug and warm, painted in the dim glow of Christmas lights, which we've decided to keep up all year.

Our friends arrive. BC friends, city friends, and most of the Hive. Over the past few months our social circles have converged, a blending of the unmarried people who still feel young.

I'm different now, but not really. I'm dating guys, but nothing else has changed—I had just been fishing in the wrong pond. I'm still the same person, just less alone.

Our deck is a swirl of snow. Across the street, squares of window light glimmer like search beacons.

Mike and Shane arrive in matching camel coats. They're still together, but they've decided to open up their relationship. It's new territory, but it seems to make them happy. Parker has started seeing an old boyfriend.

Ashley and Kirsten have settled into their new apartment and are looking forward to new beginnings. Things with Sloppy Tuna Man fizzled after the new year. Kirsten no longer sees Stefano.

Colby looks fresher, well rested for the first time since I've met him. His mother is doing better. One Saturday in October we bumped into each other on the Metro-North bound for home. He opened up to me about her illness, and I told him about my feelings for Matt.

D.Lo and Everett are still together. We think one day they'll get engaged.

I'm switching songs on my iPod when you come in. The speakers pick up the sound of the click wheel and people laugh because the technology is so outdated. I happen to look up as you walk into the kitchen.

You're a friend of a friend and you've come alone. You're looking around, terrified, trying to find the familiar face that invited you. You brought a six-pack of Brooklyn Lager, a friendly gesture. You didn't want to show up empty-handed.

Our mutual friend sees you and rescues you. She takes your Barbour coat and tosses it in the pile on the bed.

You're my opposite, with dark hair and blue eyes and a narrow nose that buttons into a heart. Somehow I can instantly tell you're gay. The sleeves of your Buffalo plaid shirt are rolled up, revealing a string bracelet affixed with a brass coin. Despite your anxiety you exude a hard-won tranquility.

You go around introducing yourself. Our mutual friend asks if you want to play beer pong and you say you do. You shake hands with my roommates and compliment our apartment. You thank them for having you. Yes, you'd love a Bud Light.

You come up to me and say hi. You tell me how much you love the song that's playing and I say it's my favorite, too. You're from New England, you live in the East Village, you work as a consultant.

I recognize what's happening, and I think back to the summer. A sudden thought of Matt slices at my heart. When you truly love someone, those feelings never go away. But I'm learning to keep them in their rightful place.

We spend a half hour talking in the corner, until someone calls us over for flip cup. As we walk to the table you place a hand on my back, just for a second, and time expands and recedes and expands again. I feel a spark, but I refuse to let myself build worlds. I've learned to protect my heart. Sure. Whatever. In the flicker of your eyes it starts. This is what I know. Our summer begins in the winter.

ACKNOWLEDGMENTS

ACKNOWLEDGMENTS

ACKNOWLEDGMENTS

ACKNOWLEDGMENTS